JESUS ASKING

J.D. WALT
JESUS ASKING
FOREWORD BY
MAXIE DUNNAM
THE THREE
TRANSFORMATIONAL
QUESTIONS OF LENT

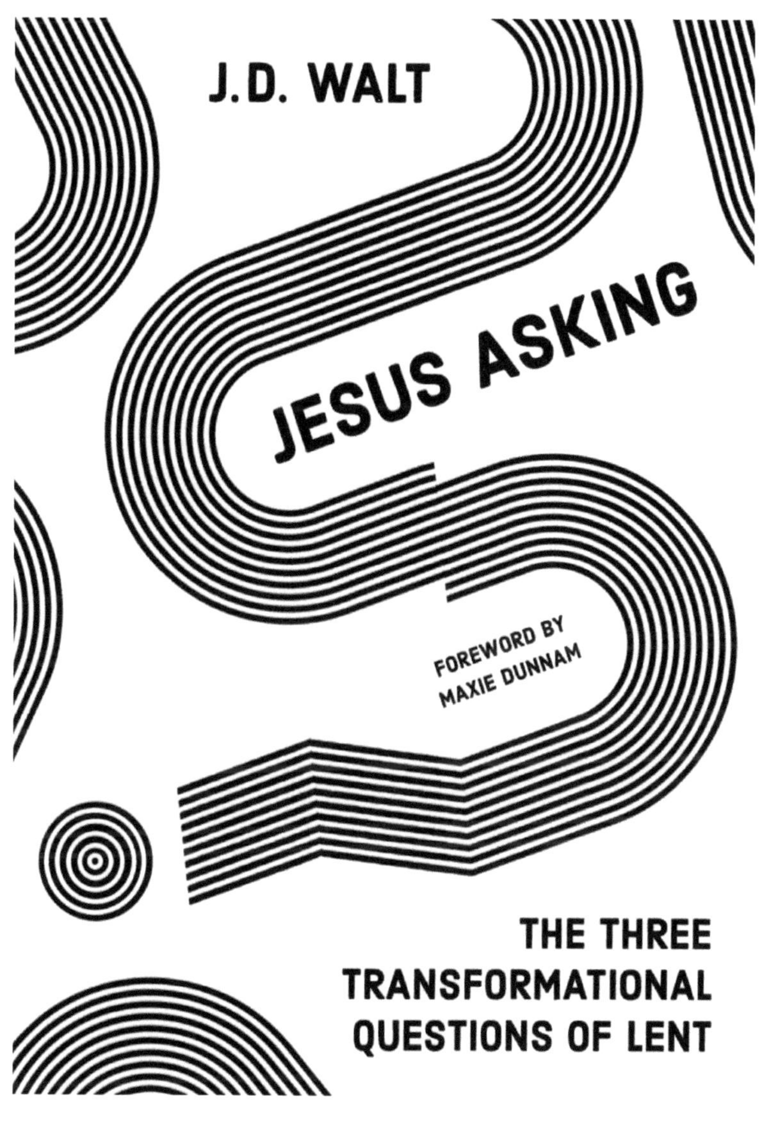

SEEDBED

Printed in the United States of America

Cover design by Faceout Studio, Kate Gendruschke
Page design and layout by PerfecType, Nashville, Tennessee

Walt, J. D. (John David)
Jesus asking : the three transformational questions of Lent / J.D. Walt Jr. – Franklin, Tennessee : Seedbed Publishing, ©2026.

pages ; cm.

ISBN 9798888002032 (paperback)
ISBN 9798888002063 (DVD)
ISBN 9798888002049 (ePub)
ISBN 9798888002056 (uPDF)
OCLC 1535932991

1. Lent--Devotional literature. 2. Lent--Prayers and devotions.
3. Lent--Meditations. 4. Spiritual exercises 5. Devotional calendars I. Title.

BV85.W3374 2026 242/.3 2025932991

SEEDBED PUBLISHING
Franklin, Tennessee
Seedbed.com

To Maxie Dunnam, my friend, mentor, father in the ministry, and the greatest Christian I have ever known. Thank you for showing me the secret.

Contents

An Invitation to Follow Jesus

This resource comes with an invitation.

The invitation is as simple as it is comprehensive. It is not an invitation to commit your life to this or that cause or to join an organization or to purchase another book. The invitation is this: to wake up to the life you always hoped was possible and the reason you were put on planet Earth.

It begins with following Jesus Christ. In case you are unaware, Jesus was born in the first century BC into a poor family from Nazareth, a small village located in what is modern-day Israel. While his birth was associated with extraordinary phenomena, we know little about his childhood. At approximately thirty years of age, Jesus began a public mission of preaching, teaching, and healing throughout the region known as Galilee. His mission was characterized by miraculous signs and wonders; extravagant care of the poor and marginalized; and multiple unconventional claims about his own identity and purpose. In short, he claimed to be the incarnate Son of God with the mission and power to save people from sin, deliver them from death, and bring them into the now and eternal kingdom of God—on earth as it is in heaven.

In the spring of his thirty-third year, during the Jewish Passover celebration, Jesus was arrested by the religious authorities, put on trial in the middle of the night, and at their urging, sentenced to death by a Roman governor. On the day known to history as Good Friday, Jesus was crucified on a Roman cross. He was buried in a borrowed tomb. On the following Sunday, according to multiple eyewitness accounts, he was physically raised from the dead. He appeared to hundreds of people, taught his disciples, and prepared for what was to come.

Forty days after the resurrection, Jesus ascended bodily into the heavens where, according to the Bible, he sits at the right hand of God, as the Lord of heaven and earth. Ten days after his ascension, in a gathering of 120 people on the day of Pentecost, a Jewish day of celebration, something truly extraordinary happened. A loud and powerful wind swept over the people gathered. Pillars of what appeared to be fire descended upon the followers of Jesus. The Holy Spirit, the presence and power of God, filled the people, and the church was born. After this, the followers of Jesus went forth and began to do the very things Jesus did—preaching, teaching, and healing—planting churches and making disciples all over the world. Today, more than two thousand years later, the movement has reached us. This is the Great Awakening and it has never stopped.

Yes, two thousand years hence and more than two billion followers of Jesus later, this awakening movement of Jesus Christ and his church stands stronger than ever. Billions of ordinary people the world over have discovered in Jesus Christ an awakened life they never imagined possible. They have overcome challenges, defeated addictions, endured untenable hardships and suffering with unexplainable joy, and stared death in the face with the joyful confidence of eternal life. They have healed the sick, gathered the outcasts, embraced the oppressed, loved the poor, contended for justice, labored for peace, cared for the dying, and, yes, even raised the dead.

We all face many challenges and problems. They are deeply personal, yet when joined together, they create enormous and complex chaos in the world, from our hearts to our homes to our churches and our cities. All of this chaos traces to two originating problems: sin and death. Sin, far beyond mere moral failure, describes the fundamental broken condition of every human being. Sin separates us from God and others, distorts and destroys our deepest identity as the image-bearers of God, and poses a fatal problem from which we cannot save ourselves. It results in an ever-diminishing quality of life and ultimately ends in eternal death. Because Jesus lived a life of sinless perfection, he is able to save us from sin and restore us to a right relationship with God, others, and ourselves. He did this through his sacrificial death on the cross on our behalf. Because Jesus rose from the dead, he is able to deliver us from death and bring us into a quality of life both eternal and unending.

This is the gospel of Jesus Christ: pardon from the penalty of sin, freedom from the power of sin, deliverance from the grip of death, and awakening to the supernatural empowerment of the Holy Spirit to live powerfully for the good of others and the glory of God. Jesus asks only that we acknowledge our broken selves as failed sinners, trust him as our Savior, and follow him as our Lord. Following Jesus does not mean an easy life; however, it does lead to a life of power and purpose, joy in the face of suffering, and profound, even world-changing, love for God and people.

All of this is admittedly a lot to take in. Remember, this is an invitation. Will you follow Jesus? Don't let the failings of his followers deter you. Come and see for yourself.

Here's a prayer to get you started:

> Our Father in heaven, it's me (say your name), I want to know you. I want to live an awakened life. I confess I am a sinner. I have failed myself,

others, and you in many ways. I know you made me for a purpose, and I want to fulfill that purpose with my one life. I want to follow Jesus Christ.

Jesus, thank you for the gift of your life and death and resurrection and ascension on my behalf. I want to walk in relationship with you as Savior and Lord. Would you lead me into the fullness and newness of life I was made for? I am ready to follow you.

Come, Holy Spirit, and fill me with the love, power, and purposes of God. I pray these things by faith in the name of Jesus, amen.

It would be our privilege to help you get started and grow deeper in this awakened life of following Jesus. For some next steps and encouragements, visit seedbed.com/awaken.

Foreword

I first met John David Walt back in 1994. I remember it because I had just been called to become the fifth president of Asbury Theological Seminary. In my first days in office, I received a handwritten letter from J. D. congratulating me on becoming the president and letting me know he would be in my first incoming class of students the following month. I, of course, wrote him back, and there began one of the beautiful friendships of my and my wife's life—now spanning more than thirty years.

Can I tell you about my second encounter with my then-new friend? I got another letter from him through the seminary post office. In the letter, he was applying to become the groundskeeper for Rose Hill, the seminary's celebrated home for its president. Soon he was riding a lawnmower in the expansive yard; raking the fallen leaves from hundreds of trees; helping my wife, Jerry, with flower gardening and all manner of horticultural pursuits; and I'll save the fishpond debacle story for another day. Yes, I take joy in remembering that J. D. Walt was my first yardman.

Early on, he approached me and asked if I would be willing to mentor him along the way in what it meant to be a minister of the gospel. Early in that journey, I introduced John David to what I considered the most important book I had written to date. It is entitled *Alive in Christ: The Dynamic Process of Spiritual Formation*. To this day, I consider it the book of my heart and core theology. I wrote it during my tenure as the world editor of the Upper Room. I'm hoping my publisher, Seedbed, will soon re-release it. If I had to summarize the book with a brief excerpt, this would be the one:

> The primary dynamic of the Christian life is abiding in Christ. Spiritual formation is "the dynamic process of receiving through faith and appropriating through commitment, discipline, and action, the living Christ into our lives to the end that our life will conform to and manifest the reality of Christ's presence in the world." (*Alive in Christ*, 26)

As we worked and walked and talked our way through this book and its accompanying workbook, J. D. took to it like a duck to water, as I had heard said in my growing-up years in Perry County, Mississippi. He was becoming more alive in Christ right before my very eyes.

This inspired me to find ways to work more directly with seminary students, which was challenging with all the administrative responsibilities required of me as president. I prayerfully decided I would develop and teach a class once each year called the Life and Work of a Minister. We worked our way through *Alive in Christ* and the *Workbook of Living Prayer,* as well as other texts. Guess who served as my first teaching assistant? Yes, my yardman, J. D. Walt. That process of working with a hundred or so students a year for those several years was one of the highlights of my tenure.

Part of that class was the exploration of the three questions J. D. introduces in this Lenten devotional book. I suppose it is why he asked me to write this foreword, which I resisted, given his extravagant dedication of the book to me. I stand by these questions and appreciate how he has built on them and made them the core dynamic of the Lenten journey to the cross.

You can only imagine the joy I now share in commending this book to you and your churches. I am proud to have been one of John David's mentors. You may not know, but after he graduated and spent some years serving the local church, I invited J. D. back to serve as dean of chapel at the seminary in the closing years of my tenure. I remain so proud of his work with our students and to now see the vibrant expression of awakening that has emerged from those years—Seedbed. And Jerry and I rarely miss a day of listening to the *Wake-Up Call*. We don't know how he does it! Well, we do. He knows the secret.

Now, I know you are wondering: What are the three questions? You will have to read on and discover them yourselves in the unfolding journey to the cross ahead of us. While the questions are helpful, they are not the secret to the Christian life.

The secret is the one to whom the questions point—Jesus Christ—and the joyful way of abiding in him and he in us. Let me close with what I consider to be the core verse of my life. It is as important and essential to me at over ninety years of age as when I first happened upon it in the robust translation of J. B. Phillips many years ago.

> The secret is simply this: Christ in you, yes Christ in you, bringing with him the hope of all the glorious things to come! (Col. 1:27)

Joy and peace,
Maxie D. Dunnam
Ash Wednesday 2025

In the past God spoke to our ancestors through the prophets at many times and in various ways, but in these last days he has spoken to us by his Son, whom he appointed heir of all things, and through whom also he made the universe. The Son is the radiance of God's glory and the exact representation of his being, sustaining all things by his powerful word. After he had provided purification for sins, he sat down at the right hand of the Majesty in heaven.

—Hebrews 1:1–3

Ash Wednesday, Day 1

Welcome to the Forty Days of Lent

CONSECRATE

Wake up, sleeper, rise from the dead,
and Christ will shine on you. (Eph. 5:14)

Jesus, I belong to you.
I lift up my heart to you.
I set my mind on you.
I fix my eyes on you.
I offer my body to you as a living sacrifice.
Jesus, we belong to you.
Praying in the name of the Father and of the Son and of the Holy Spirit, amen.

READ

Galatians 4:4–5 NASB

But when the fullness of the time came, God sent His Son, born of a woman, born under the Law, so that He might redeem those who were under the Law, that we might receive the adoption as sons and daughters.

CONSIDER

Lent. The word comes from an old Anglo-Saxon word, *lencten*, which means "lengthen." It is a word that signifies springtime—when the days begin to lengthen. Seems pretty harmless and benign. It's spring again. Big deal, right? It's another lap around the sun, another walk through the cycle of seasons—winter, spring, summer, and fall. They come like clockwork, don't they? In fact, they *are* clockwork. This is how time moves. The Bible calls this kind of time *chronos*, the Greek root found in our English word *chronological*. Winter. Spring. Summer. Fall.

The Bible also speaks of another kind of time: *kairos*. In short, kairos time is God time, which is not so much about time as it is about God. In fact, God dwells outside time in the realm of eternity. And this is precisely the amazing thing about God time. God time is the reality that happens when eternity breaks into time. This, of course, is the story of Jesus.

But when the fullness of the time came, God sent His Son, born of a woman, born under the Law, so that He might redeem those who were under the Law, that we might receive the adoption as sons and daughters.

Chronos time is measured by seasons and kept on a calendar. Kairos time is marked by a story and kept by a community. That means the most important timepiece we have is not a calendar or a clock but the Bible—the revealed Word of God.

We don't need more shifting seasons; we need more movement. We don't need more religion; we need more life. We don't need more activity; we need more awakening. We don't need more answers; we actually need more questions.

Here is the meaning of the movement of Lent. In the thirty-third spring of the first millennium, Jesus of Nazareth began a descent from the Mount of Transfiguration deep into the Valley of the Cross, where he would die a death by crucifixion and rise from the dead as the ultimate act of love to reconcile the lost human race to the God who created us.

Beginning today—Ash Wednesday—Lent is a journey of forty days ending on Holy Saturday and culminating with Easter Sunday. The six intervening Sundays do not count in the forty days. Since the resurrection of Jesus

Christ from the dead—on Easter Sunday—Sundays have been for feasting, never fasting.

Lent is an invitation to break the predictable pace of another trip around the sun and to get in step with the movement of the story of Jesus. It is an opportunity to wake up to the reality of the real, true, and living God in real, true, and living time. It's why I always like to say: *Wake up, sleeper, rise from the dead, and Christ will shine on you!*

One final note as we embark. This is not a book of answers, but one of questions. It will unfold as a journey of questions. Early on we will touch on what I call "the question of all questions." It will take a few weeks of walking together, but we will arrive at what I call "the three transformational questions." And be warned, they are deep questions, and the depth at which you are willing to engage them will determine the depth of growth you can expect on the other side. Now, one final question on this first day of the journey: Are you ready?

PRAY

Our Father, thank you for your Son, Jesus. Lord Jesus, we step into these forty days of Lent eager to follow you, to walk in your ways, to discover your will, and to awaken to new life in you. Come, Holy Spirit! Where you lead us, we will follow. We are ready. Praying in Jesus's name, amen.

JOURNAL

What are your intentions as we walk into these forty days of Lent? What are your hopes? What are your questions?

Thursday, Day 2

On Pulling the Fire Alarm in Church

CONSECRATE

Wake up, sleeper, rise from the dead,
and Christ will shine on you. (Eph. 5:14)

Jesus, I belong to you.
I lift up my heart to you.
I set my mind on you.
I fix my eyes on you.
I offer my body to you as a living sacrifice.
Jesus, we belong to you.
Praying in the name of the Father and of the Son and of the Holy Spirit, amen.

READ

Joel 2:1 NASB

Blow a trumpet in Zion,
And sound an alarm on My holy mountain!
Let all the inhabitants of the land tremble,
For the day of the LORD *is coming;*
Indeed, it is near.

CONSIDER

Years ago I served as dean of the chapel at Asbury Theological Seminary. I often did confounding things. One I always wanted to do but never did was to pull the fire alarm in the chapel during a worship service. I always wanted to do it on Ash Wednesday, the solemn assembly that opens the door into the movement of Lent.

"Why?" you ask? Because that's what the prophet is doing in today's text, which is the traditional, classic text for the opening of Lent. Didn't he say "sound an alarm"?

Blow a trumpet in Zion,
And sound an alarm on My holy mountain!

I once had a friend, Ricky, who was straight out of the Old Testament—a spitfire prophet type. He told me how he walked up to a lost and broken friend's door one day and greeted him with these words, "Bobby, if I was driving by and your house was on fire, would you want me to stop and tell you?"

The friend said, “Of course, I would!”

Ricky then said, “Well, Bobby, your house is on fire!” It was Ricky’s way of pulling the fire alarm.

Friends, I’m no doomsday prophet, but I am a bit of a truth teller. Have you looked around lately? Our house is on fire. I don’t need to rehearse the story with you. And isn’t that part of the problem? Like the proverbial frog in the kettle, we’ve slowly accepted the disastrous status quo all around us. We feel powerless to effect meaningful change, and we often retreat into the enclaves of resistance we call churches or, worse, political parties. Plenty of people are pulling the fire alarm and pointing at all the problems *out there*.

But that won’t fix the problem. We must pull the fire alarm *in here*. Awakening starts with me. How might I pull the fire alarm in my own heart? Here’s how the prophet Joel says to do it:

> “Yet even now,” declares the Lord,
> “Return to Me with all your heart,
> And with fasting, weeping, and mourning;
> And tear your heart and not merely your
> garments.”
> Now return to the Lord your God,
> For He is gracious and compassionate,
> Slow to anger, abounding in mercy
> And relenting of catastrophe. (Joel 2:12–13 NASB)

Those seven words show us how to break the glass: "Return to Me with all your heart."

PRAY

Our Father, thank you for your Son, Jesus. Lord Jesus, we're sorry for locating the problem out there and absolving ourselves of any real responsibility. We want to confess, the problem is in here, in our hearts. We are part of the problem. We know it even if we do not feel it. And we can't fix it. It's why we want to return to you with all our hearts. Thank you for accepting them in broken pieces. Come, Holy Spirit! Praying in Jesus's name, amen.

JOURNAL

What are some of the broken pieces of your heart? What keeps you from simply and humbly offering them back to Jesus? Are you letting a part of your broken heart keep you from returning to him with *all* your heart?

Friday, Day 3

I Have Cancer and You Do Too

CONSECRATE

Wake up, sleeper, rise from the dead,
and Christ will shine on you. (Eph. 5:14)

Jesus, I belong to you.
I lift up my heart to you.
I set my mind on you.
I fix my eyes on you.
I offer my body to you as a living sacrifice.
Jesus, we belong to you.
Praying in the name of the Father and of the Son and of the Holy Spirit, amen.

READ

Joel 2:12–13 NASB

"Yet even now," declares the LORD,
"Return to Me with all your heart,
And with fasting, weeping, and mourning;
And tear your heart and not merely your garments."
Now return to the LORD your God,
For He is gracious and compassionate,
Slow to anger, abounding in mercy
And relenting of catastrophe.

CONSIDER

I always wanted to break the glass and pull the fire alarm in the chapel on Ash Wednesday, but I never did. I sort of did it once. And I never really recovered from the debacle it unleashed.

I stood up before the chapel, and as I began my message, I said I had some bad news I needed to share first. "I'm sad to tell you," I said, "but I have recently learned that I have cancer." There were gasps and even a shriek, and some began to cry. I then tried to qualify my declaration by saying that I didn't have cancer like they thought. I had a different sort of cancer, and they had it too. I told them that we all have sin cancer. And, yes, it is terminal.

Isn't that the point of Ash Wednesday? We get the sign of the cross made on our foreheads in black ashes. We hear the words spoken straight into our souls: "From dust you have come, and to dust you shall return. Repent and believe the gospel."

That's more than a message that none of us is getting out of here alive. It's worse than that. We are already dead. We have sin cancer, and it's terminal. We've had it from birth.

However, there is really good news. That's what *gospel* means: good news. The gospel is that there is a cure, and it has a 100-percent cure rate. The cure has a name: Jesus. We will get into how the cure works in the coming days, but for now you just need to know that Jesus cures sin cancer—and not just a little bit. It's not only an after-you-die-you-will-go-to-heaven cure. That's true, but the cure actually touches every aspect of your life right here and now. And what is the word that invites this transformational cure? It is *repent*, and it means exactly what the Scripture text says today:

"Return to Me with all your heart."

And what about *believe*, the other command from our Ash Wednesday liturgy? *Believe* doesn't mean just accept it. *Believe* means lean in with your whole weight.

Do you remember what the name *Jesus* means? It means "he will save his people from their sins" (Matt. 1:21).

It means 100-percent cure.

PRAY

Our Father, thank you for your Son, Jesus. Lord Jesus, the song is right. There is just something about your name. You are the cure for sin cancer. And as much as we hate to admit it, we have it. So instead of admitting it, we will confess it. We are sinners. We have sin cancer. We need you, Jesus, to cure us. But we want you to know this, Jesus: We want you. Come, Holy Spirit. Praying in Jesus's name, amen.

JOURNAL

Are you aware that you have a bigger problem than your pesky sins, which are symptoms? Are you aware of the sin-cancer tumor that is causing those symptoms? How does this metaphor help you better understand Jesus as the cure for our condition? And how does this differ from simply dealing with the symptoms of the sickness?

Saturday, Day 4

On Metastatic Sin Cancer

CONSECRATE

Wake up, sleeper, rise from the dead,
and Christ will shine on you. (Eph. 5:14)

Jesus, I belong to you.
I lift up my heart to you.
I set my mind on you.
I fix my eyes on you.
I offer my body to you as a living sacrifice.
Jesus, we belong to you.
Praying in the name of the Father and of the Son and of the Holy Spirit, amen.

READ

Genesis 1:27

So God created mankind in his own image,
in the image of God he created them;
male and female he created them.

CONSIDER

The Bible tells us that when God first created human beings, he made us in his very image. "Made in God's image" is a phrase bandied about so much in Christian circles it has become cliché. This truth is actually mind-blowing. To bear the image of your Creator means when other people see you, they see your Creator.

Clearly something went wrong somewhere because, Toto, we aren't living in that Kansas anymore. What went wrong is both simple and complex. Our ancient forebears, the original humans—the prototypes—turned against God. They wanted to be their own gods. This broke the bonded relationship and resulted not in the loss of God's image but in the loss of God's presence with us, effectively rendering the image of God broken and bankrupt.

To continue our cancer metaphor: Think of the image of God as a super internal (albeit unseen) organ of sorts—not just existing at the very core of our being but running throughout our whole body and connected with every other system and organ in our body. Think of this super organ as the system that infuses and profuses divine DNA (a.k.a. the eternal life) throughout our bodies. And it doesn't just course through our bodies, it also connects our beings and bodies together in a supernaturally extraordinary way. The image of God is the touchpoint and interface where we know and experience abiding union with God and with others created in God's image.

When our ancient forebears willfully broke the covenantal relationship with God and rebelliously hid and turned against one another and blamed each other for their failure, thereby claiming victimhood, the image of God was not removed but rendered null and inoperable. It was like a cancer entered our genetic code and decimated the image of God from the inside out. Eternal life was gone. Not only was our quality of life greatly diminished, but our quantity of life was severely limited. With sin came death.

What's important to understand is that we didn't start the fire. It was already burning when we got here. It seems unfair, and perhaps it is, but those are the simple facts. Let's be clear. We didn't initially cause the problem. However, we were born with the problem. And, yes, we have contributed to it in such a way that it is immaterial that it didn't actually begin with us.

Let's give Paul the last word on this today: "Therefore, just as through one man sin entered into the world, and death through sin, and so death spread to all mankind, because all sinned—" (Rom. 5:12 NASB).

That's the biblical definition of metastatic sin cancer. And I know—I can't let that hanging dash hang. So now to the gospel, which is the good news of the cure: "For as through the one man's disobedience the many were made sinners, so also through the obedience of the One the many will be made righteous" (v. 19 NASB).

PRAY

Our Father, thank you for your Son, Jesus. Lord Jesus, we know we didn't cause the problem, but we now have the problem of sin and death, and therefore, we are part of the problem. We are sorry for the ways we have misunderstood this and responded poorly as a result. We want your image to be fully restored in us so we might live life to the fullest for your glory, for others' gain, and for our good. Come, Holy Spirit, and teach and train us in the cure of this gospel. Praying in Jesus's name, amen.

JOURNAL

What do you make of this way of imagining the image of God in us? Does it resonate? Where do you struggle with or push back against it? What are the implications of it?

First Sunday of Lent

When Jesus came to the region of Caesarea Philippi, he asked his disciples, "Who do people say the Son of Man is?"

They replied, "Some say John the Baptist; others say Elijah; and still others, Jeremiah or one of the prophets."

"But what about you?" he asked. "Who do you say I am?"

Simon Peter answered, "You are the Messiah, the Son of the living God."

Jesus replied, "Blessed are you, Simon son of Jonah, for this was not revealed to you by flesh and blood, but by my Father in heaven. And I tell you that you are Peter, and on this rock I will build my church, and the gates of Hades will not overcome it. I will give you the keys of the kingdom of heaven; whatever you bind on earth will be bound in heaven, and whatever you loose on earth will be loosed in heaven." Then he ordered his disciples not to tell anyone that he was the Messiah.

From that time on Jesus began to explain to his disciples that he must go to Jerusalem and suffer many things at the hands of the elders, the chief priests and the teachers of the law, and that he must be killed and on the third day be raised to life.

Peter took him aside and began to rebuke him. "Never, Lord!" he said. "This shall never happen to you!"

Jesus turned and said to Peter, "Get behind me, Satan! You are a stumbling block to me; you do not have in mind the concerns of God, but merely human concerns."

Then Jesus said to his disciples, "Whoever wants to be my disciple must deny themselves and take up their cross and follow me. For whoever wants to save their life will lose it, but whoever loses their life for me will find it. What good will it be for someone to gain the whole world, yet forfeit their soul? Or what can anyone give in exchange for their soul? For the Son of Man is going to come in his Father's glory with his angels, and then he will reward each person according to what they have done.

"Truly I tell you, some who are standing here will not taste death before they see the Son of Man coming in his kingdom."

—Matthew 16:13–28

Monday, Day 5

We Sin Because We Are Sinners

CONSECRATE

Wake up, sleeper, rise from the dead,
and Christ will shine on you. (Eph. 5:14)

Jesus, I belong to you.
I lift up my heart to you.
I set my mind on you.
I fix my eyes on you.
I offer my body to you as a living sacrifice.
Jesus, we belong to you.
Praying in the name of the Father and of the Son and of the Holy Spirit, amen.

READ

Romans 5:19 NASB

For as through the one man's disobedience the many were made sinners, so also through the obedience of the One the many will be made righteous.

CONSIDER

As we delve further into this movement we call Lent, which is the movement from death to life, we need to make sure we have clarity on the core fundamentals. We began with the fundamental of the original image of God, something none of us has known or experienced because of the failure of our ancient forebears. We were all born into the failure of fallenness. It is so important to understand that we are not fallen creatures because of our failures. It is actually the opposite. We fail because of our fallenness. In fact, short of some kind of miraculous intervention we can't not fail.

Let's try this another way. There is sickness and then there are symptoms of the sickness. The sickness in this instance is capital-S Sin. It is fallenness, the condition into which we were born. The symptoms of this sickness are little-s sins. Our sins are our failures. So let me ask you this question: Do the symptoms come from the sickness, or does the sickness come from the symptoms? Of course, the symptoms come from the sickness. If the sickness can be cured, the symptoms will subside.

Here's the point. We are not sinners because we sin. We sin because we are sinners. We are not fallen because we fail. We fail because we are fallen. It follows, then, that we must treat the sickness rather than try to endlessly manage the symptoms. We must deal with the condition of our fallenness rather than endlessly try to mitigate our failures.

Trying harder to do better may manage and even mask the symptoms, but it will not cure the sickness. We need a much deeper treatment.

For as through the one man's disobedience the many were made sinners . . .

We were born with the cancer of Adam.

. . . so also through the obedience of the One the many will be made righteous.

The real problem comes when we spend all our energy trying to treat the symptoms. Sin is not a moral failure. It is a complete system failure. This system failure creates many varied moral failures, but we must understand that these failures, while problematic, are not the real problem. Sin is the big problem. Our sins are the problems stemming from the big problem of our Sin.

Jesus is the cure for the capital-S cancer of Sin. We can only be cured by the chemotherapy of the blood of Jesus and the radiating glory of his righteousness.

It's why the Bible says things like this:

> For God so loved the world that he gave his one and only Son, that whoever believes in him shall not perish but have eternal life. For God did not send his Son into the world to condemn the world, but to save the world through him. (John 3:16–17)

> For our sake he made him to be sin who knew no sin, so that in him we might become the righteousness of God. (2 Cor. 5:21 ESV)

PRAY

Our Father, thank you for your Son, Jesus. Lord Jesus, we're tired of treating the symptoms of Sin. We want you to treat the sickness of Sin. We receive your sacrificial life, death, and resurrection for our Sin and for our sins. We receive you, our cure. Holy Spirit, would you deepen our salvation, our healing? Praying in Jesus's name, amen.

JOURNAL

Have you, like me, misunderstood Sin and sins? Do you see how our status as sinners is inherited before it is earned and how salvation cannot be worked for and earned—only given and received?

Tuesday, Day 6

The Question of All Questions

CONSECRATE

Wake up, sleeper, rise from the dead,
and Christ will shine on you. (Eph. 5:14)

Jesus, I belong to you.
I lift up my heart to you.
I set my mind on you.
I fix my eyes on you.
I offer my body to you as a living sacrifice.
Jesus, we belong to you.
Praying in the name of the Father and of the Son and of the Holy Spirit, amen.

READ

Mark 8:27–29

Jesus and his disciples went on to the villages around Caesarea Philippi. On the way he asked them, "Who do people say I am?"

They replied, "Some say John the Baptist; others say Elijah; and still others, one of the prophets."

"But what about you?" he asked. "Who do you say I am?" Peter answered, "You are the Messiah."

CONSIDER

There were six of them—five girls and one boy. They ranged in age from twelve to fifteen. We sat around the table on a Sunday morning in a classroom in the Gillett Methodist Church. It was the first day of our first confirmation class, the first one I had ever taught since my own confirmation many years before.

For those unfamiliar, confirmation is a rite of passage where a person (most often a young person) walks through a transformational learning process designed to lead them to an opportunity to give their lives to Jesus Christ, thereby confirming their personal faith in him as Savior and Lord.

I didn't start with a curriculum or even much of a plan. I wasn't interested in giving them religious instruction or denominational indoctrination. Those things aren't wrong, of course, but I felt we needed to be far more basic and fundamental. We needed an extended conversation about first things.

I passed out six blank moleskin-type books, designating them as our confirmation journals. I asked this group of young people to open the books and to write on the inside cover, in large print, what I called "the question of all questions."

The question of all questions comes from Jesus of Nazareth.

It is addressed to every person who ever lived and who ever will live.

He asked the question for the first time of his disciples in a place known as Caesarea Philippi, north of Galilee. There is an alternate name for this place: Pan. *Pan* means "many"—as in, many gods. Pan was also home to an ancient shrine known as the Gates of Hades.

Here's the scene: The place is crawling with people. They are congregating around this shrine and that one and clustering around this guru and that teacher. It's kind of like a national park for religious business. I picture Jesus's disciples gathered around him as they look at this scene.

That's the setup for the question of all questions. It wasn't the first question he asked that day though. Here was the first question:

"Who do people say I am?"

They replied, "Some say John the Baptist; others say Elijah; and still others, one of the prophets."

Then he dropped the mother of all questions on them:

"But what about you?" he asked. "Who do you say I am?"

So, I said to my first-ever confirmation class, the five girls and one boy seated around the table, "Write those six words in large, bold letters inside the front cover of your confirmation journal. That's the question of all questions and the focus of our class over these next months."

And now I say it to you as we walk these forty days of Lent together with Jesus to the cross.

"But what about you?" he asked. "Who do you say I am?"

PRAY

Our Father, thank you for your Son, Jesus. Lord Jesus, thank you for cutting to the chase. Thank you for speaking plainly and from your heart to ours. Mostly, thank you for caring enough to ask us the question, "Who do you say I am?" We don't want to give you a pat answer. We will live with the question in a deeper way. Come, Holy Spirit, and grant us a fresh revelation that we might make a real response. Praying in your name, amen.

JOURNAL

Do you see how it is possible to get the answer biblically and doctrinally correct and yet still miss the point? How might that be avoided?

Wednesday, Day 7

From Believing in God to Believing God

CONSECRATE

Wake up, sleeper, rise from the dead,
and Christ will shine on you. (Eph. 5:14)

Jesus, I belong to you.
I lift up my heart to you.
I set my mind on you.
I fix my eyes on you.
I offer my body to you as a living sacrifice.
Jesus, we belong to you.
Praying in the name of the Father and of the Son and of the Holy Spirit, amen.

READ

Mark 8:29

"But what about you?" he asked. "Who do you say I am?" Peter answered, "You are the Messiah."

CONSIDER

In the early days of the church, the forty days before the day of resurrection were set apart for training and preparing new Christians for baptism. Over the years, the church began to call these baptismal candidates a strange term: *catechumens*.

This word comes from the term *catechesis*. Catechesis is biblical and doctrinal instruction given to candidates preparing for baptism or confirmation. It is based on what is called a catechism, which is a long series of questions and answers. So reviewing, confirmation is the process of catechumens going through the process of catechesis by learning the answers to a long series of biblical and doctrinal questions accomplished by engaging (and often memorizing) a catechism.

Now, here's what I know: A person can learn all the answers to all the questions and still fail the test. Take it a step further. A person can make an A on the test and still fail the class. In fact, if a person knows all the answers to all the questions but still misses the answer to the question of all questions, all their learning will have been for naught. You remember the question of all questions, right?

"But what about you? . . . Who do you say that I am?"

You see, all the answers to all the questions of catechumens and catechesis and catechism are good. We might even say they are essential. However, they can so easily fall short of what Jesus might call "the only necessary thing." Why? Because all the answers to all the questions keep us in the place of believing things about God. They can keep us focused on the preliminary question, "Who do people say I am?"—which is another way of asking, "What do other people believe about me?"

So, the only necessary thing comes down to the only necessary question. It will be the question at the starting line and at the finish line.

"But what about you? . . . Who do you say that I am?"

It's not, "Do you believe in God?"

It is much deeper than that. The question is: "Do you believe God?"

A sick person is cured not by believing in the medicine but by taking it.

We are not saved from the curse of Sin and the problem of our sins by mentally assenting to biblical doctrine. We are not saved by trying harder to be better so that we might somehow overcome our unsolvable problem. We are saved by grace through faith in the atoning life, death, resurrection, ascension, and coming return of Jesus Christ.

PRAY

Our Father, thank you for your Son, Jesus. Lord Jesus, your gift to us of yourself came at an unimaginable cost and is an unspeakable joy. Would you awaken us, by the Holy Spirit, to grasp higher, deeper, wider, and longer for an understanding beyond our natural capacities—that we could know this gift in our heart of hearts? Praying in Jesus's name, amen.

JOURNAL

Have you thought of Sin and sins in the framework of sickness and symptoms before? How does it help you better understand the fallen condition of human beings and the cure?

Thursday, Day 8

It's Your Turn

CONSECRATE

Wake up, sleeper, rise from the dead,
and Christ will shine on you. (Eph. 5:14)

Jesus, I belong to you.
I lift up my heart to you.
I set my mind on you.
I fix my eyes on you.
I offer my body to you as a living sacrifice.
Jesus, we belong to you.
Praying in the name of the Father and of the Son and of the Holy Spirit, amen.

READ

Matthew 16:16

Simon Peter answered, "You are the Messiah, the Son of the living God."

CONSIDER

"But what about you? Who do you say that I am?"

I know. This is the third day I've asked this question. Why?

Because it is the question of all questions.

And because it is a question whose answer is meant to grow larger and more expansive with every passing year. But here's something I have discovered, and I suspect you have too: Just because we are growing more in our knowledge about Jesus doesn't mean we are growing to know Jesus more.

Most of us have been well-trained in an approach to education that focuses on building knowledge. We love facts and data and information, and we have gathered a lot of it over the years, even when it comes to God. Certainly, knowledge about God and the Bible is a good thing, but it is not the main thing. The Bible is clear. The goal is not to amass knowledge about something. The goal is to grow in knowing someone—namely, Jesus.

It's why Jesus comes close, maybe too close for comfort. I picture him putting his hands on each of my shoulders as he looks into my eyes and asks me—up close and personal—"But what about you, John David? Who do you say that I am?"

He's not looking for me to recall what it might say on his "About" page. He's not asking for a recital of the Apostles' Creed. He's not looking for an affirmation of faith. He's looking for a demonstration of faith. He wants to know where we are in our relationship. It's like he's asking, "Who am I in relationship to you?" He is asking you and me to define the relationship based on how we know him.

That day at Caesarea Philippi Jesus was not talking to the crowds but to the Twelve. He was not looking for a group response but a personal revelation. We get the impression Peter all but lunged forward with his exuberant response:

Simon Peter answered, "You are the Messiah, the Son of the living God."

Peter was not giving Jesus a textbook answer but a transformational affirmation. It was coming not from a place of information but from revelation. We get the impression Jesus all but lunged forward with his exclamatory reply: "Jesus replied, 'Blessed are you, Simon son of Jonah, for this was not revealed to you by flesh and blood, but by my Father in heaven'" (Matt. 16:17).

Peter had given Jesus not an affirmation of the information of faith but an activation of the revelation of faith itself.

So here we are, face-to-face with Jesus. His hands are on our shoulders. He knows us. And he loves us. But he wants to know where we are with him. What is the nature of the relationship? Where is our faith? "Who am I to you?" he humbly asks.

"But what about you, [insert your name]? Who do you say that I am?"

Remember, he's seeking not your knowledge but your knowing, not information but revelation, not the answer of your head but the response of your heart.

Okay, I'll go first.

PRAY

Our Father, thank you for your Son, Jesus. Lord Jesus, you are the one who never leaves. You are our light and our life. You are our Savior and our Lord. You are our all in all; indeed, our reason for living. You are our source and strength, our joy in sadness, and our peace in anxiety. You are our reason. Praying in your name, amen.

JOURNAL

Your turn. How do you respond to Jesus's question: "But what about you? Who do you say that I am?"

Friday, Day 9

From Information to Revelation

CONSECRATE

Wake up, sleeper, rise from the dead,
and Christ will shine on you. (Eph. 5:14)

Jesus, I belong to you.
I lift up my heart to you.
I set my mind on you.
I fix my eyes on you.
I offer my body to you as a living sacrifice.
Jesus, we belong to you.
Praying in the name of the Father and of the Son and of the Holy Spirit, amen.

READ

Matthew 16:18

And I tell you that you are Peter, and on this rock I will build my church, and the gates of Hades will not overcome it.

CONSIDER

In my first year of law school I met my favorite law professor. For my money, Dr. Robert Laurence was the Master Yoda of law professors. One day in the midst of an insanely complex property law class, in trying to get across a concept which was deeply logical yet defied logic, he said this: "One page of history is worth more than ten thousand pages of logic." In legal terms he was trying to help our obtuse black-and-white minds grasp something of the relationship between common-law precedent and statutory law—between what actually happened and what should have happened.

Here's what I heard: Life trumps theory. Real-world experience is more valuable than theoretical preparation. In those days I was struggling deeply with Jesus as I perceived he was calling me away from a career in the law and into the fields of amazing grace. I had no playbook for that, no history or logic to bring to bear. In those days, in the spirit of Professor Laurence's dictum, I experienced my own flash of insight along those same lines:

A word of revelation is worth more than ten thousand pages of information.

When it comes to Jesus, and particularly when it comes to answering the question of all questions, what we need is not more information but more revelation. Isn't this what so excited Jesus that day in Caesarea Philippi with his band of disciples? "Jesus replied, 'Blessed are you, Simon son of Jonah, for this was not revealed to you by flesh and blood, but by my Father in heaven'" (Matt. 16:17).

This is what I wanted for my first-ever confirmation class. I wanted them to learn—and to learn to learn—by revelation, not just by information. This meant we would need to trade the pursuit of knowledge for the passion of knowing.

Isn't this precisely what Paul was praying for his little churches back in the day? "I keep asking that the God of our Lord Jesus Christ, the glorious Father, may give you the Spirit of wisdom and revelation, so that you may know him better" (Eph. 1:17).

Something tells me you are ready for this. You are tired of going from one Bible study to the next. You are more than a little weary of learning more things about Jesus. You want to actually know him better. And you've come to the realization that this will require less of you and yet more of you at the same time. You are going to have to shift gears.

You will need to shift out of the gear of striving and into the gear of surrender—less taking on and more letting go.

That's enough to process today. Less is more. Letting go of taking more on is better. And in the spirit of Professor Laurence's dictum, let's give the psalmist the last word today: "Better is one day in your courts than a thousand elsewhere" (Ps. 84:10a).

PRAY

Our Father, thank you for your Son, Jesus. Lord Jesus, we confess, we like information. We like right answers. We like to ace the quiz. We want to learn how to learn by revelation. Come, Holy Spirit, and break through, leading us into the way of knowing you beyond mere knowledge. Praying in your name, amen.

JOURNAL

What will it take for you to press past the comfort zone of more information and knowledge and into the realm of revelation and knowing? What in you resists this kind of move?

Saturday, Day 10

For the Love of a Krispy Kreme Doughnut

CONSECRATE

Wake up, sleeper, rise from the dead,
and Christ will shine on you. (Eph. 5:14)

Jesus, I belong to you.
I lift up my heart to you.
I set my mind on you.
I fix my eyes on you.
I offer my body to you as a living sacrifice.
Jesus, we belong to you.
Praying in the name of the Father and of the Son and of the Holy Spirit, amen.

READ

Psalm 34:8

Taste and see that the Lord is good;
blessed is the one who takes refuge in him.

CONSIDER

I am always trying to help people understand and appropriate the difference between knowledge and knowing and between religious practices and a relationship with God. Draw two similar overlapping circles. Label the left circle "knowledge" and the right circle "knowing." Now the question to you: What would you label the overlap?

To make this point come alive, some years ago I decided to pull a stunt in one of my sermons. I'm not given to gimmicks, but I am always down for a good stunt. I was preaching a sermon on one of my favorite biblical texts, Philippians 3:10–11, which says: "I want to know Christ—yes, to know the power of his resurrection and participation in his sufferings, becoming like him in his death, and so, somehow, attaining to the resurrection from the dead."

I took with me into the pulpit a dozen fresh and hot Krispy Kreme doughnuts. Everyone oohed and aahed over them as I cracked open the box and unveiled them to the congregation. When I asked, "Who wants a doughnut?" every hand in the room shot to the ceiling. I took a single doughnut from the box and began my sermon.

Here was my text: "I want to know a Krispy Kreme doughnut."

I lifted the doughnut to my mouth as though I were going to take a bite but stopped short. And then, as I lowered the doughnut, I began to recount for the congregation the origin story of doughnuts—how fried dough has ancient antecedents; how the doughnut as we know it originated with the Dutch as olykoeks (or oily cakes), which were more like doughnut holes; how the Dutch brought them to America in the seventeenth century; and how the ring shape came into being and so forth.

Then I paused for dramatic effect and lifted the doughnut to my mouth again, opening wide, only to stop short and then lower the doughnut again. I reached for my text again: "I want to know a Krispy Kreme doughnut, and the power of its sugary confectionary delight."

I launched into a compelling depiction of the process used by Krispy Kreme to make its delectable sugary glaze—how it's made from powdered sugar, milk, and vanilla extract and brought to the exact consistency required for it to flow like a river across the "glazing waterfall" and onto the crispy baked confections passing underneath.

Again, in what must have felt like slow motion, I pulled the doughnut to my open mouth and even pressed it past my lips and under my teeth, where I held it suspended for several seconds. As I stopped short of biting into the doughnut and pulled it away, people throughout the room let out an audible gasp of agonizing frustration. "Eat it!" someone shouted.

"I want to know a Krispy Kreme doughnut, and the power of its sugary confectionary delight, and the fellowship of sharing in its nutritional sufferings, becoming like it in its fat gram measurement and its caloric count."

Taking the doughnut in both hands, I lifted it up and broke it apart, playfully mimicking the gesture used in the rite of holy Communion. Again, I inhaled the sweet aroma of the sugary fried bread and offered it outwardly to the congregation. The room lost its mind at this point.

And then I read, with dramatic pace and effect, the real text of the day: "I want to know Christ—yes, to know the power of his resurrection and participation in his sufferings, becoming like him in his death, and so, somehow, attaining to the resurrection from the dead."

And then I recited the text of Psalm 34:8:

Taste and see that the L*ORD* *is good;*
blessed is the one who takes refuge in him.

And then I lifted the doughnut and took a massive bite, and the house filled with joyful shouts and thunderous applause as the ecstatic delight on my face completed the story.

PRAY

Our Father, thank you for your Son, Jesus. Lord Jesus, you are good beyond belief and better than the best. Your life is truly life, and your presence is everything. To know you is to love you, and to love you is to know you more. Come, Holy Spirit, and set our knowledge on fire until it becomes knowing you. Praying in your name, amen.

JOURNAL

So back to the two overlapping circles. What would you label the overlap? I'll share my answer in Monday's entry.

Second Sunday of Lent

After six days Jesus took with him Peter, James and John the brother of James, and led them up a high mountain by themselves. There he was transfigured before them. His face shone like the sun, and his clothes became as white as the light. Just then there appeared before them Moses and Elijah, talking with Jesus.

Peter said to Jesus, "Lord, it is good for us to be here. If you wish, I will put up three shelters—one for you, one for Moses and one for Elijah."

While he was still speaking, a bright cloud covered them, and a voice from the cloud said, "This is my Son, whom I love; with him I am well pleased. Listen to him!"

When the disciples heard this, they fell facedown to the ground, terrified. But Jesus came and touched them. "Get up," he said. "Don't be afraid." When they looked up, they saw no one except Jesus.

As they were coming down the mountain, Jesus instructed them, "Don't tell anyone what you have seen, until the Son of Man has been raised from the dead."

—Matthew 17:1–9

Monday, Day 11

More to This Life

CONSECRATE

Wake up, sleeper, rise from the dead,
and Christ will shine on you. (Eph. 5:14)

Jesus, I belong to you.
I lift up my heart to you.
I set my mind on you.
I fix my eyes on you.
I offer my body to you as a living sacrifice.
Jesus, we belong to you.
Praying in the name of the Father and of the Son and of the Holy Spirit, amen.

READ

Philippians 3:10–11

I want to know Christ—yes, to know the power of his resurrection and participation in his sufferings, becoming like him in his death, and so, somehow, attaining to the resurrection from the dead

CONSIDER

I'm still thinking about the overlap of those two circles from last week. You too? Remember, we labeled the left-hand circle "knowledge" and the right-hand circle "knowing." Of course, there are other possible labels. Here are a few:

Information/Revelation
Religious Practices/Experienced Relationship
PhD in Doughnut-ology/Six Doughnuts Later
Knowing About Jesus/Actually Knowing Jesus

So here's how I would label the overlap between the two circles: *awakening*.

I still remember it like it was yesterday. It was back in my law school days when I was searching for the way forward. I was driving down a country road with the windows down (probably because I was running out of gas and needed to turn the air conditioner off). Steven Curtis Chapman's song "More to This Life" came on the radio.

In it, he reflects on watching people walk by and seeing an emptiness in their eyes.

The lyrics deeply resonated with me and reflected what I was seeing around me. Everyone and everything around me seemed to lack meaning and purpose and destiny. Most people around me were just trying to keep up, while the rest of them labored to get ahead. *But for what?* I kept asking myself. They had lost the movement of life and were just going through the motions of it all. That's when I heard the chorus, which cries out that there is more to this life than just getting by.

This song became the seed of my awakening.

I had been in church all my life, appreciative of it yet not markedly impacted by it. I had enough knowledge about God, and I had religious practices. The problem I had is I only knew what I knew. I knew going to church and reading my Bible (or at least a shallow devotional most mornings). I knew trying harder to do more to be better. I knew what most people I knew knew—a form of religion without the power.

The other problem I had is I did not know what I didn't know. I didn't have a category for a real, living, and dynamic relationship with God or an experiential faith or the dramatic reality of knowing Jesus and the power of his resurrection or most of the things the New Testament describes as the Christian faith.

Something tells me at least some of you know exactly what I am talking about and more of you once camped out there for longer than you care to remember.

There's another word I might suggest for the overlap. It's the condition preceding the reality of awakening: *holy discontent*. (I know, that's two words.) Holy discontent is the sense of having a splinter in your soul. It's what awakened in me that day I was driving down a country road and heard that song, "More to This Life."

But the bigger question is: "So what?"

So what if there were more to this life, even your life? More than just more of what you already have and know. Would you want it?

PRAY

Our Father, thank you for your Son, Jesus. Lord Jesus, you are the more to this life. And we want more of you. Come, Holy Spirit, and fully awaken me to the more that you have for me. Praying in Jesus's name, amen.

JOURNAL

Have you ever sensed, or do you now, that there is more to life than you presently know or experience? Where have you sought to find that more? Could it be Jesus for you?

Tuesday, Day 12

What Happens on Transfiguration Mountain?

CONSECRATE

Wake up, sleeper, rise from the dead,
and Christ will shine on you. (Eph. 5:14)

Jesus, I belong to you.
I lift up my heart to you.
I set my mind on you.
I fix my eyes on you.
I offer my body to you as a living sacrifice.
Jesus, we belong to you.
Praying in the name of the Father and of the Son and of the Holy Spirit, amen.

READ

Mark 9:2

After six days Jesus took Peter, James and John with him and led them up a high mountain, where they were all alone. There he was transfigured before them.

CONSIDER

Let's start with theology. Lent begins on Ash Wednesday and the big problem of the human race: sin and death. We come to the altar and hear the dreadful-hopeful words, "From dust you have come, and to dust you will return. Repent and believe the gospel." We were never meant to sin, and we were never meant to die, but because our ancient forebears chose to rebel against God, they experienced the consequence, which is death. And they passed it on to us. Though we inherited the curse, we have added to the dark legacy, and hence we mark our foreheads on Ash Wednesday with the ashen cross.

But there's a better starting place than theology. It's geography. While Lent's theological beginning is Ash Wednesday, its geographical beginning precedes it. While the theology of Lent begins in the dark valley of the shadow of death, the geography of Lent begins on a high mountain with transcendent light.

After six days Jesus took Peter, James and John with him and led them up a high mountain, where they were all alone. There he was transfigured before them.

I always thought of the transfiguration as a one-and-done, one-off kind of happening meant only for the Son of God. In other words, I didn't see any personal application—until I looked deeper. The Greek word that we translate as the English word *transfiguration* is transliterated as *metamorphoō* (pronounced "meh-tah-mor-FOH-oh"). It means something like "to change form in keeping with inner reality." With his transfiguration, it is as though Jesus pulled back the veil of his human form and revealed to us the divine substance underneath.

Metamorphoō.

You are already making the connection to the English word *metamorphosis*. The word signifies change but not ordinary change. It means change of another order of magnitude. When I made this connection, I realized the transfiguration was not a one-and-done, one-off, Jesus-only occasion. He was showing us his intentions for our lives. The great church father Athanasius is said to have put it this way: "Jesus became like us so that we could become like him."

He took on our form in order to make us into his form. And herein lies the meaning of *metamorphoō*. It is transformation. *Trans + formation.* Transcendent formation. It is change of another order of magnitude.

On the Mount of Transfiguration, Jesus unveils and reveals to us what we are meant to become—ordinary human beings invested and infused with the transcendent presence of God.

How does this happen? This is the journey of Lent. We follow Jesus on the way to the cross. The journey begins at the top of Transfiguration Mountain, and it leads to the bottom of the world—to the very foot of the cross.

PRAY

Our Father, thank you for your Son, Jesus. Lord Jesus, we must have this transfiguration—transcendent formation. And yet we know the only way to have this is to have you. To know you is to love you, and to love you is to become like you, to be remade in your image. Lead us in this way. We will follow. Praying in your name, amen.

JOURNAL

How have you thought about this occasion we call the transfiguration? Have you ever considered what Jesus may have been revealing to us about ourselves and our possibilities?

Wednesday, Day 13

Why Not Be Completely Changed into Fire?

CONSECRATE

Wake up, sleeper, rise from the dead,
and Christ will shine on you. (Eph. 5:14)

Jesus, I belong to you.
I lift up my heart to you.
I set my mind on you.
I fix my eyes on you.
I offer my body to you as a living sacrifice.
Jesus, we belong to you.
Praying in the name of the Father and of the Son and of the Holy Spirit, amen.

READ

Exodus 3:1

Now Moses was tending the flock of Jethro his father-in-law, the priest of Midian, and he led the flock to the far side of the wilderness and came to Horeb, the mountain of God.

CONSIDER

Remember our watchword for the week: *metamorphoō*.

Sometimes it takes getting a little ways down the mountain to fully take in what we saw on the summit. I picture us still in a bit of stunned silence as we walk down the trail. We want to talk, but we don't quite know what to say. It's like we saw Jesus turn completely into fire. Here's the mystery though: He was on fire, but he was not burning up. And then we remember this:

> Now Moses was tending the flock of Jethro his father-in-law, the priest of Midian, and he led the flock to the far side of the wilderness and came to Horeb, the mountain of God. There the angel of the LORD appeared to him in flames of fire from within a bush. Moses saw that though the bush was on fire it did not burn up. (Ex. 3:1–2)

When we recall those eleven words, "though the bush was on fire it did not burn up," we know that's exactly what we witnessed. And then I remember this story from the Desert Fathers:

One day Abbot Lot went to see his teacher, Abbot Joseph, and Abbot Lot said, "Abbot Joseph, the best that I am able, I keep my little fast, my little rule, my little devotions. To the best that I am able, I keep my meditation and my prayer, and I try to cleanse my heart of earthly desires, but Abbot Joseph, it is not enough. I still haven't found what I seek."

Now Abbot Joseph listened closely to his student, and when Abbot Lot was done speaking, Abbot Joseph got up out of his chair, and he reached his arms and his hands up into the air until he stretched out each of his ten fingers, and out of the tips of each of his fingers shot pure flame—ten burning candles there in the middle of the desert—and Abbot Joseph said to Abbot Lot, "Why not be completely changed into fire?"

Now, as we descend the mountain, you ask, "Do you think Jesus wants to transform us into burning bushes?"

And I say, "Yes, I think Jesus wants to transform us into burning bushes—on fire but not burning up." Lent is the journey of transformation, of reversal even, in which we are turned from ashes into fire.

And you ask, "So how does Jesus do this?"

And I say, "Remember our watchword for the week: *metamorphoō*."

And we keep walking down the mountain.

PRAY

Our Father, thank you for your Son, Jesus. Lord Jesus, you are fire. You are the fire. And if you are in us, that makes us fire. Would you lead us on this way of being completely changed into fire, being transformed into your image? It will be for your glory, for others' gain, and for our good. Praying in your name, amen.

JOURNAL

So the question to you is: Why not be completely changed into fire? Would you want that?

Thursday, Day 14

How Do I "Be Transformed"?

CONSECRATE

Wake up, sleeper, rise from the dead,
and Christ will shine on you. (Eph. 5:14)

Jesus, I belong to you.
I lift up my heart to you.
I set my mind on you.
I fix my eyes on you.
I offer my body to you as a living sacrifice.
Jesus, we belong to you.
Praying in the name of the Father and of the Son and of the Holy Spirit, amen.

READ

Romans 12:2

Do not conform to the pattern of this world, but be transformed by the renewing of your mind. Then you will be able to test and approve what God's will is—his good, pleasing and perfect will.

CONSIDER

Remember our watchword for the week: *metamorphoō*.

As I said earlier, I always thought the transfiguration was a one-off, one-of-its-kind event that was just for Jesus and, consequently, really had no personal or practical application as it related to us.

Boy, was I wrong.

I've done a little digging. I looked up our watchword *metamorphoō*. In addition to its appearance in the gospel accounts, it appears in two other verses. And did I mention those two verses are what I would call power texts? I'll share the first one today and the next one tomorrow.

Do not conform to the pattern of this world, but be transformed by the renewing of your mind. Then you will be able to test and approve what God's will is—his good, pleasing and perfect will.

And there it is, hiding like an Easter egg, under the words "be transformed": *metamorphoō*.

Notice how the verse begins with "Do not," and yet it doesn't go on to give us something we can do for ourselves. That's hard for people like us who like to have a to-do list. Transformation is not something we do, is it? It is not a set of activities or duties or disciplines or responsibilities we take on.

Transformation is someone we become. And notice the root word of that word *become*. It is *be*. Now put it together. The meaning of our watchword, *metamorphoō*, is "be transformed." Transformation is not a good person becoming a better person. It's a dead person becoming a truly alive person.

So transformation is not something we do to ourselves. Does that mean it is something that happens to us? Because that still sounds like we have to do something to make it happen. But what if transformation is not something but Someone that happens to us—even more so, in us?

That would change everything, wouldn't it? And isn't that exactly the point of *metamorphoō*—changing everything?

So maybe instead of asking, "What do I need to do?" we should ask, "How can I be transformed?"

PRAY

Our Father, thank you for your Son, Jesus. Lord Jesus, we ask you, "How can we be transformed?" And we sense you are saying, “Follow me. Belong to me. Behold me.” This is the way. Jesus, we belong to you. Come, Holy Spirit, and lead us in this way of transformation. Praying in Jesus’s name, amen.

JOURNAL

Are you willing to let go of your need to change yourself? Are you ready to abandon the program of self-improvement? Are you ready for Jesus to take the wheel, for real transformation?

Friday, Day 15

Why Consecration Is the Doorway to Transformation

CONSECRATE

Wake up, sleeper, rise from the dead,
and Christ will shine on you. (Eph. 5:14)

Jesus, I belong to you.
I lift up my heart to you.
I set my mind on you.
I fix my eyes on you.
I offer my body to you as a living sacrifice.
Jesus, we belong to you.
Praying in the name of the Father and of the Son and of
the Holy Spirit, amen.

READ

Romans 12:1

Therefore, I urge you, brothers and sisters, in view of God's mercy, to offer your bodies as a living sacrifice, holy and pleasing to God—this is your true and proper worship.

CONSIDER

Albert Einstein was once famously asked this question: "Dr. Einstein, if you were told the world were coming to an end and you had one hour to come up with a solution to save it, how would you spend that hour?"

He is said to have wryly replied, "I would spend fifty-five minutes trying to define the question and five minutes solving it."

It strikes me that religion and religious enterprising spend all their energy frenetically engineering solutions to problems that turn out not to be the real problems after all. We readily focus on managing the symptoms instead of curing the sickness. We pay the high interest rate but do not focus on paying down the actual debt. We endlessly focus on reading the thermometer instead of trying to get our hands on the thermostat. We try harder and harder to do more and more to be better and better rather than doing the only necessary thing, which would lead to being transformed.

So in the spirit of defining the problem, here's where we landed: Transformation is not a problem to be solved but a Person to be encountered. It is not something we do to ourselves but Someone who happens to and in us. The question is not "What do I need to do?" It is "How can I be transformed?"

Often the answer to one verse in the Bible can be found in the verse that comes just before or after it. The answer to the question of the text is found in the context. Remember, we have been dealing with the second verse of the twelfth chapter of Romans. The first verse of the twelfth chapter of Romans holds the key:

Therefore, I urge you, brothers and sisters, in view of God's mercy, to offer your bodies as a living sacrifice, holy and pleasing to God—this is your true and proper worship.

Did you see it? Three words capture the secret to our watchword, *metamorphoō*, which you remember means "be transformed."

Offer your bodies.

It sounds too simple, doesn't it? Maybe that's why it's so easy to miss it. We busy ourselves with all manner of activity aimed at God, intended to try to make ourselves better or to increase our level of commitment. But what if Jesus isn't looking for our commitment? What if he's looking for something more simple and basic and humble?

Offer your bodies as a living sacrifice.

There's a word for this invitation: *consecration.* Consecration is a way of showing up before God that says simply and humbly, "I'm here and I'm yours."

We've already been praying it every single day here. I thought it was time we talked about it.

Jesus, I belong to you.

PRAY

Our Father, thank you for your Son, Jesus. Lord Jesus, we said it earlier today, but now we say it again: We belong to you. And we hear you say back, "I belong to you." And that means everything. Come, Holy Spirit, and lead us into deep consecration, the kind that leads to transformation. Praying in Jesus's name, amen.

JOURNAL

How do you view the difference between commitment and consecration?

Saturday, Day 16

Commitment vs. Consecration

CONSECRATE

Wake up, sleeper, rise from the dead,
and Christ will shine on you. (Eph. 5:14)

Jesus, I belong to you.
I lift up my heart to you.
I set my mind on you.
I fix my eyes on you.
I offer my body to you as a living sacrifice.
Jesus, we belong to you.
Praying in the name of the Father and of the Son and of the Holy Spirit, amen.

READ

Luke 10:41–42

"Martha, Martha," the Lord answered, "you are worried and upset about many things, but few things are needed—or indeed only one. Mary has chosen what is better, and it will not be taken away from her."

CONSIDER

In this legendary story, which of course is true and not to be confused as a legend, we witness the difference between more commitment and deeper consecration. Let's dive into the story.

"As Jesus and his disciples were on their way, he came to a village where a woman named Martha opened her home to him" (Luke 10:38).

Something we should notice about Jesus: Everywhere he goes he's needed, and he is always glad to meet the needs of so many people. In this story we see what he wants most. Jesus wants to be wanted. He is like us in this way. We are glad to go where we are needed, but what we really desire is to go where we are wanted. Jesus goes where he is wanted.

"She had a sister called Mary, who sat at the Lord's feet listening to what he said" (v. 39).

Martha wanted Jesus to come to her home. Mary wanted Jesus.

"But Martha was distracted by all the preparations that had to be made" (v. 40a).

Martha was preparing her home. Mary was preparing her heart.

Martha was distracted. Mary was devoted.

"She came to him and asked, 'Lord, don't you care that my sister has left me to do the work by myself? Tell her to help me!'" (v. 40b).

Martha is mad, but she doesn't know why. She's mad at Jesus. "You don't care," she says. She's mad at Mary. "My irresponsible sister couldn't care less." She's really mad at herself, because her life is not working for her. She needs Jesus to fix it. And he does.

"Martha, Martha," the Lord answered.

He calls her name twice—as if to say, "I see you, dear daughter." Then he goes in deeper, way past her distractions and into her true condition:

"You are worried and upset about many things."

"I know you are tired, weary, and carrying heavy burdens. This is your way, your comfort zone. And it's not that you want out of it. You just want your sister to be in it with you. You are not comfortable with the fact that your sister has left the comfort zone and the predicable place of busyness and overfunctioning and the easy distractibility of trying to please others, to make everyone happy, to check the boxes so others will accept and approve her."

Martha instructs Jesus to tell Mary to come to her side.

Jesus invites Martha to come to Mary's side.

"But few things are needed—or indeed only one. Mary has chosen what is better, and it will not be taken away from her."

Martha was committed. Mary was consecrated.

This is the only necessary thing.

PRAY

Our Father, thank you for your Son, Jesus. Lord Jesus, we confess, so often we are worried and upset about many things. We want to learn the way to the only necessary thing, living a consecrated life of belonging to you. Holy Spirit, would you awaken and lead us in this way? Praying in Jesus's name, amen.

JOURNAL

Are you seeing the difference between being more committed and being more deeply consecrated? What is the difference?

Third Sunday of Lent

Then Jesus came from Galilee to the Jordan to be baptized by John. But John tried to deter him, saying, "I need to be baptized by you, and do you come to me?"

Jesus replied, "Let it be so now; it is proper for us to do this to fulfill all righteousness." Then John consented.

As soon as Jesus was baptized, he went up out of the water. At that moment heaven was opened, and he saw the Spirit of God descending like a dove and alighting on him. And a voice from heaven said, "This is my Son, whom I love; with him I am well pleased."

Then Jesus was led by the Spirit into the wilderness to be tempted by the devil. After fasting forty days and forty nights, he was hungry. The tempter came to him and said, "If you are the Son of God, tell these stones to become bread."

Jesus answered, "It is written: 'Man shall not live on bread alone, but on every word that comes from the mouth of God.'"

—Matthew 3:13–4:4

Abruptly Jesus broke into prayer: "Thank you, Father, Lord of heaven and earth. You've concealed your ways from sophisticates and know-it-alls, but spelled them out clearly to ordinary people. Yes, Father, that's the way you like to work."

Jesus resumed talking to the people, but now tenderly. "The Father has given me all these things to do and say. This is a unique Father-Son operation, coming out of Father and Son intimacies and knowledge. No one knows the Son the way the Father does, nor the Father the way the Son does. But I'm not keeping it to myself; I'm ready to go over it line by line with anyone willing to listen.

"Are you tired? Worn out? Burned out on religion? Come to me. Get away with me and you'll recover your life. I'll show you how to take a real rest. Walk with me and work with me—watch how I do it. Learn the unforced rhythms of grace. I won't lay anything heavy or ill-fitting on you. Keep company with me and you'll learn to live freely and lightly."

—Matthew 11:25–30 (MSG)

Monday, Day 17

From Many Things to One Thing

CONSECRATE

Wake up, sleeper, rise from the dead,
and Christ will shine on you. (Eph. 5:14)

Jesus, I belong to you.
I lift up my heart to you.
I set my mind on you.
I fix my eyes on you.
I offer my body to you as a living sacrifice.
Jesus, we belong to you.
Praying in the name of the Father and of the Son and of the Holy Spirit, amen.

READ

Matthew 11:28–30

Come to me, all you who are weary and burdened, and I will give you rest. Take my yoke upon you and learn from me, for I am gentle and humble in heart, and you will find rest for your souls. For my yoke is easy and my burden is light.

CONSIDER

Jesus's words to Martha still echo today—only they aren't echoes. They are the piercing plea from the heart of God to the hearts of Mary and Martha and you and me. "The Lord answered, 'Martha, Martha! You are worried and upset about so many things, but only one thing is necessary. Mary has chosen what is best, and it will not be taken away from her'" (Luke 10:41–42 CEV).

I am worried and upset about so many things. You too? I see you. You are carrying a lot these days. And you are not carrying just what's on your list today. You are carrying disappointment and pain and frustration over things not working out like they should have yesterday or you had hoped they would twenty years ago. You are carrying the burdens of others and their frustrations and feelings. You are weary of the enormous responsibility you feel to hold it all together and somehow make it work.

And what once felt like faith now feels like another list of religious responsibilities that you're not fulfilling—not praying enough, not fasting at all, not going to church on Sunday mornings because of the kids' sports games, not giving enough money—and you're feeling the constant onslaught of oughts and shoulds to try harder to do more to be better, to measure up.

Could Jesus be talking to you? Because I'm almost positive he's talking to me. Hear him out:

> Are you tired? Worn out? Burned out on religion? Come to me. Get away with me and you'll recover your life. I'll show you how to take a real rest. Walk with me and work with me—watch how I do it. Learn the unforced rhythms of grace. I won't lay anything heavy or ill-fitting on you. Keep company with me and you'll learn to live freely and lightly. (Matt. 11:28–30 MSG)

Now insert your name in this passage and speak these words aloud so your ears can hear them:

> [Say your name, say your name!], you are worried and upset about so many things, but only one thing is necessary. Mary has chosen what is best, and it will not be taken away from her. (adapted from Luke 10:41–42 CEV)

Our deep inner rumblings of holy discontent are the birth pangs of consecration that lead to transformation. We want the only necessary thing, but we aren't quite sure what to do with the many things. Jesus is right now speaking three simple words to you: "Come to me."

Don't worry about the many things. Make the move toward consecration that will lead to transformation. Turn your eyes upon Jesus. I want you to see yourself sitting there on the floor, right at his feet. Now hear Jesus speaking this word aloud (through your voice) concerning you: "[Say your name] has chosen what is best, and it will not be taken away from them."

PRAY

Our Father, thank you for your Son, Jesus. Lord Jesus, we are ready for the one thing, the only necessary thing. We know it will cost us our focus on so many things. We know the many things will not go away, but they will lose our commitment. By the power of the Holy Spirit, we are choosing consecration. Praying in Jesus's name, amen.

JOURNAL

Are you seeing the parallels between the movement from many things to one thing and the movement from slavery to freedom? What might the easy yoke of Jesus be like?

Tuesday, Day 18

From Priorities to Priority

CONSECRATE

Wake up, sleeper, rise from the dead,
and Christ will shine on you. (Eph. 5:14)

Jesus, I belong to you.
I lift up my heart to you.
I set my mind on you.
I fix my eyes on you.
I offer my body to you as a living sacrifice.
Jesus, we belong to you.
Praying in the name of the Father and of the Son and of the Holy Spirit, amen.

READ

Matthew 6:33
But seek first his kingdom and his righteousness, and all these things will be given to you as well.

CONSIDER

We left off yesterday with you sitting on the floor at the feet of Jesus. Let me remind you what he was saying:

"[Insert your name] has chosen what is best, and it will not be taken away from them."

Now, I know what you are thinking. *What about the many things I still have on my plate? They didn't go away.* Correct, and they won't go away. And if anything, the more you yield yourself to Jesus, the more you will experience even more things getting added to the many things. Jesus holds enormous gravity, and the more he is in you, the more gravity you will have. The change you need is a change in your relationship to all the things. This change won't come with a better task-management system or a new getting-things-done approach. This change will only come as we change our relationship with the one thing—the only necessary thing—Jesus.

It is precisely at this point where we make a left turn when we must make a right turn. The wrong turn looks like this way of thinking: *I need to be less like Martha and more like Mary.* This is not a story about Martha and Mary. This is a story about Jesus.

These are not personality types as some want to think, with Martha being the doer type and Mary the contemplative type. No, this is a story about the only necessary thing. This is a story about the core matter of priority. And notice I did not say "priorities." This is one of the more absurd words of our time: *priorities. Priority* means "first." It comes from the word *prior*, which means "to go before." Only one thing can be first. To say we have priorities categorically means we have no priority. This is why Martha is "worried and upset about many things" (Luke 10:41).

Martha has priorities. Mary has a priority.

So how do we change our relationship with the many things always swirling around and about us? We must change our relationship with the one necessary thing: our proximity to Jesus.

Why are we worried and upset about many things? It's an important question we will save for tomorrow. Today we must focus on the one thing, the priority. Hear Jesus out on the priority:

But seek first his kingdom and his righteousness, and all these things will be given to you as well.

Did you see what Jesus just did there? He gave us the priority. He gave us a first only. There is no second. And then in the span of eleven words—"and all these things will be added to you as well"—he changed our relationship to "all these things."

Remember where you are? You are still sitting at the feet of Jesus. Ponder this offer Jesus is making, this exchange of the many things for the only necessary thing. It's real.

PRAY

Our Father, thank you for your Son, Jesus. Lord Jesus, we have many priorities. We want one priority. You are the priority. Something tells us you will take care of the many things if we can just choose you. This is our consecration. Praying in Jesus's name, amen.

JOURNAL

What do you make of this notion of the absurdity of multiple priorities? Do you see it? How might Jesus become the priority, even in the midst of the many things?

Wednesday, Day 19

His Baptism Is My Baptism Too

CONSECRATE

Wake up, sleeper, rise from the dead,
and Christ will shine on you. (Eph. 5:14)

Jesus, I belong to you.
I lift up my heart to you.
I set my mind on you.
I fix my eyes on you.
I offer my body to you as a living sacrifice.
Jesus, we belong to you.
Praying in the name of the Father and of the Son and of the Holy Spirit, amen.

READ

Matthew 4:1–3

Then Jesus was led by the Spirit into the wilderness to be tempted by the devil. After fasting forty days and forty nights, he was hungry. The tempter came to him and said, "If you are the Son of God, tell these stones to become bread."

CONSIDER

The forty days of Lent, in the classical sense, are meant to help us identify with Jesus as he spent forty days in the wilderness being tempted by Satan. This focus, while appropriate, has led to many adventures in missing the point. Growing up, we were taught to deny ourselves something we enjoyed, like chocolate, until Easter, at which point we would gorge ourselves on chocolate until we were sick. As a result, I understood fasting as a misery to endure rather than a mystery to engage.

Many years later I am only beginning to grasp the fasting way of Jesus. Fasting is a way of bringing to the surface the broken attachments of our deep identity so that we might be healed. Watch how the story unfolds:

After fasting forty days and forty nights, he was hungry.

Now notice the shape of the temptation. Satan attacks Jesus at the point of his (and our) greatest vulnerability: his identity while he's in a weakened, famished condition.

The tempter came to him and said, "If you are the Son of God, tell these stones to become bread."

In other words, "If you are who you say you are, use your power to manipulate your situation. Prove yourself by your performance. Validate your own identity." Notice how Jesus turns the table on the tempter and identifies the only necessary thing in the situation.

"Jesus answered, 'It is written: "Man shall not live on bread alone, but on every word that comes from the mouth of God"'" (Matt. 4:4).

Here's where it gets interesting. Do you remember the last word that came from the mouth of God? It happened at Jesus's baptism in the Jordan River, just before he was led by the Holy Spirit into the desert.

As Jesus came up out of the water, the Holy Spirit descended. "And a voice from heaven said, 'This is my Son, whom I love; with him I am well pleased'" (Matt. 3:17).

Jesus's identity had been established firmly by the Word of God in the power of the Spirit of God.

One of Satan's greatest strategies to keep us upset and worried about many things is to convince us we must perform in order to be affirmed and accepted. God, our Father, gave Jesus, his Son, the performance review before the job ever started. Jesus was living his life and doing his work not *for* acceptance but *from* acceptance.

Jesus lived his life and did his work from a bonded attachment to his Father through the active power of the Word of God and the abiding presence of the Spirit of God. This is the only necessary thing.

PRAY

Father, thank you for your Son, Jesus. Lord Jesus, we receive your baptism and those blessing words from our Father: "My son/daughter, my beloved, with you I am well pleased." Yes and amen. We receive the deep acceptance and abiding affirmation of our Father. Thank you for your baptism. By your Spirit, we will feast on the Father's blessing words. Praying in Jesus's name, amen.

JOURNAL

Have you ever considered that Jesus's baptism is your baptism too? Can you receive this baptismal blessing freely as gift? Will you find ways to affirm it regularly? Daily?

Thursday, Day 20

Receiving the Deep Approval of God

CONSECRATE

Wake up, sleeper, rise from the dead,
and Christ will shine on you. (Eph. 5:14)

Jesus, I belong to you.
I lift up my heart to you.
I set my mind on you.
I fix my eyes on you.
I offer my body to you as a living sacrifice.
Jesus, we belong to you.
Praying in the name of the Father and of the Son and of the Holy Spirit, amen.

READ

Matthew 3:16–17

As soon as Jesus was baptized, he went up out of the water. At that moment heaven was opened, and he saw the Spirit of God descending like a dove and alighting on him. And a voice from heaven said, "This is my Son, whom I love; with him I am well pleased."

CONSIDER

Why was Jesus baptized? He didn't need to be baptized for himself. He certainly didn't need John's baptism of repentance from sin. Jesus was baptized for our sake. He did it for us. He did it, as he told his cousin, John, "to fulfill all righteousness" (Matt. 3:15). He was showing us what it means to "seek first the kingdom of God and his righteousness, and all these things will be added to you" (Matt. 6:33 ESV).

He stepped into the river and transformed a ritual of repentance into a tidal wave of righteousness. But what does that word mean—*righteousness*? We assume we know, until we are asked. It feels to us like a religious word that means something like "perfect behavior," like "never doing anything wrong." It's why Jesus being baptized seems wrong to us. He was already perfect. However, this is not what the Bible means by *righteousness*.

The Greek word is *dikaiosuné* (pronounced "dee-kah-yos-oo'-nay"). It essentially means "the approval of God."

And there we have it. Baptism is not something we do in order to be approved. It is something we do because we are approved. Righteousness does not come from following the rules but from coming to know the Ruler.

In so many relationships in life, we find we have to change and even conform in order to be accepted. The opposite is true. We have to be accepted in order to truly change. Sure, anyone can manage a little behavior conformation to get by, but that's not what God has in mind for his children. He wants deep-hearted healing. He wants us to "be transformed," as the Scripture says, "by the renewing of [our] mind[s]" (Rom. 12:2). In fact, he wants to do the transformation himself, by his presence within us. First, we must receive his deep acceptance of us as his sons and daughters—just as we are, in our brokenness. Only then can we begin to grow into the fullness of the men and women he made us to be.

Remember, if someone says you have to change in order to be approved and loved, that's a lie. You will change only when you know you are approved and loved. That's why over and over the Bible repeats things like this: "But God demonstrates his own love for us in this: While we were still sinners, Christ died for us" (Rom. 5:8).

Jesus got into the water that day and heard these words of divine approval spoken over his whole life so we could hear these words of divine approval spoken over our broken lives: "[Insert your name], you are my son/daughter, my beloved one. With you I am well pleased."

As you sit at the feet of Jesus, could you just let that wash over you today?

PRAY

Our Father, thank you for your Son, Jesus. Lord Jesus, thank you for the way you fulfilled "all righteousness" and for making it your gift to us. Come, Holy Spirit, and activate this deep approval of God for us in our lives. Praying in Jesus's name, amen.

JOURNAL

How have you worked for approval from God and from other people to try to gain righteousness? Are you ready for the shift to a righteousness that can't be earned but only received as a gift by faith? Are you ready to receive approval from God and to work *from* this approval rather than *for* it?

Friday, Day 21

Jesus Likes You

CONSECRATE

Wake up, sleeper, rise from the dead,
and Christ will shine on you. (Eph. 5:14)

Jesus, I belong to you.
I lift up my heart to you.
I set my mind on you.
I fix my eyes on you.
I offer my body to you as a living sacrifice.
Jesus, we belong to you.
Praying in the name of the Father and of the Son and of the Holy Spirit, amen.

READ

Matthew 3:17

And a voice from heaven said, "This is my Son, whom I love; with him I am well pleased."

CONSIDER

Years ago, I found myself way over my head in a situation way beyond my pay grade. I was the pastor to the speakers and worship leaders for One Day, a massive solemn assembly of college students. As tens of thousands of them camped out in the surrounding fields, awaiting the coming day, the leaders met together for a time of consecration. Let's just say I was the only one in the who's who circle of leaders you had never heard of. And it was my job to lead them.

Over the next couple of hours I prayed for these leaders and anointed them one by one. As we finished up, a young prophet type, Neil, approached me. He motioned for me to hand him the anointing oil, invited me to kneel, and began to anoint and pray for me. I got low to the ground, bracing for a stern word from this man known for speaking the straight, hard truth.

I'll never forget what he prayed over me, because it changed my life forever.

He said, "John David, you need to know that Jesus loves you, but you need to know more than that. Maybe you think he has to love you because he's Jesus. He does love you, but you need to know that Jesus also likes you. He enjoys you. He likes being around you. He likes you so much that he considers you a friend. And there's one more thing you need to know. Jesus loves you. Jesus likes you. And Jesus wants you to know that he's proud of you."

Something broke in me that night. It was my brokenness. I realized I was still trying to please God. That night, I received the blessing of knowing in a deep place that God was already pleased with me.

And then it hit me. This is the Father's blessing over you and me from the baptism of Jesus.

You are my son/daughter: I love you.

You are my beloved: I like you.

With you I am well pleased: And I'm proud of you.

Everything I thought I understood about consecration shifted that night. I had thought about consecration as my initiative to show God I was serious about him. I realized it was God's initiative to show me he was serious about me. I had thought of consecration as my commitment to God. I learned instead it was God's commitment to me.

That was the beginning of a change that is still changing me. It will change you too.

PRAY

Our Father, thank you for your Son, Jesus. Lord Jesus, how can we thank you for the blessing of your baptism and for making it our baptism too? By your poured-out Spirit, we are washed by your favor, blessed by your affection, and delighted by your joy in and over and through us. Praying in your name, amen.

JOURNAL

Have you received the blessing of these words—that the God who made you not only loves you but also likes you, and not only does he like you but he's also proud of you?

Saturday, Day 22

What Are We?

CONSECRATE

Wake up, sleeper, rise from the dead,
and Christ will shine on you. (Eph. 5:14)

Jesus, I belong to you.
I lift up my heart to you.
I set my mind on you.
I fix my eyes on you.
I offer my body to you as a living sacrifice.
Jesus, we belong to you.
Praying in the name of the Father and of the Son and of the Holy Spirit, amen.

READ

Genesis 1:27

So God created mankind in his own image,
in the image of God he created them;
male and female he created them.

CONSIDER

In my job as a pastor in a rural area, I work with people of all ages. We are truly an intergenerational church, not because we try to be but because we can't help it, and because we can't afford the kind of staffing it takes to split everyone up into age-level groupings. I am the only official employee. That makes me the youth pastor and the children's pastor and the senior adults pastor and on it goes.

In my work with our students and their friends, I have been reminded of something I learned from my own children in their growing-up years. It is this: Kids have no idea who they are. They are carrying enormous levels of anxiety and stress. They are trying to measure up to impossible standards while fitting into a toxic culture no one can authentically belong to.

And I know what you are thinking. *They don't know who they are because they don't know Whose they are.* While that sounds good and seems right, it's kind of a cliché, and kids these days can smell a cliché from a mile away. I decided to take a different approach with the kids at our church. I decided to start by teaching them not *who* they were but what they *are*.

Since we are learning by revelation, we don't start with biology but theology. Theology informs biology, not the other way around. The core revelation of *what* we are comes in the very first chapter of the Bible. It happened on the sixth day, after God had made everything else in creation.

So God created mankind in his own image,
in the image of God he created them;
male and female he created them.

We know the image of God is not our human form because at creation God was not yet human. The image of God was our divine substance. We were not created as gods but as image-bearers of God. So, what is the image of God?

The kids and I followed the trail of revelation to Psalm 8, where we see these words: "What is mankind that you are mindful of them, human beings that you care for them? You have made them a little lower than the angels and crowned them with glory and honor" (vv. 4–5).

What are we? We are image-bearers of the one true and living God. We are a phylum below the classification of angels. We are crowned with glory and honor. Here's how I translate that for our kids and for you and me:

What am I? What are you?

I am an unbelievable, inconceivable, unrepeatable miracle of God!

PRAY

Our Father, thank you for your Son, Jesus. Lord Jesus, we are made in your image. We are made a little lower than angelic beings. Like you, we are an unbelievable, inconceivable, unrepeatable miracle of God. By your Spirit cause me to believe this at the deepest level and so live. Praying in your name, amen.

JOURNAL

Have you ever considered the question "What are you?" How do you respond?

Fourth Sunday of Lent

The Son is the image of the invisible God, the firstborn over all creation. For in him all things were created: things in heaven and on earth, visible and invisible, whether thrones or powers or rulers or authorities; all things have been created through him and for him. He is before all things, and in him all things hold together. And he is the head of the body, the church; he is the beginning and the firstborn from among the dead, so that in everything he might have the supremacy. For God was pleased to have all his fullness dwell in him, and through him to reconcile to himself all things, whether things on earth or things in heaven, by making peace through his blood, shed on the cross.

Once you were alienated from God and were enemies in your minds because of your evil behavior. But now he has reconciled you by Christ's physical body through death to present you holy in his sight, without blemish and free from accusation—if you continue in your faith, established and firm, and do not move from the hope held out in the gospel. This is the gospel that you heard and that has been proclaimed to every creature under heaven, and of which I, Paul, have become a servant.

—Colossians 1:15–23

Monday, Day 23

The Flux Capacitor

CONSECRATE

Wake up, sleeper, rise from the dead,
and Christ will shine on you. (Eph. 5:14)

Jesus, I belong to you.
I lift up my heart to you.
I set my mind on you.
I fix my eyes on you.
I offer my body to you as a living sacrifice.
Jesus, we belong to you.
Praying in the name of the Father and of the Son and of the Holy Spirit, amen.

READD

Psalm 139:13–14

For you created my inmost being;
you knit me together in my mother's womb.
I praise you because I am fearfully and wonderfully made;
your works are wonderful,
I know that full well.

CONSIDER

The other day I did something I never imagined I would do. I went on Amazon and I ordered a flux capacitor. Yep, you read that right, a flux capacitor. For those of you perhaps too old or too young to get the reference, back in the late 1900s a very popular series of movies came out called *Back to the Future*. At the center of the story was the age-old quest of time travel—more specifically, the attempt to go back into the past and adjust something that happened in history in order to thereby change the future.

A mad scientist of sorts (Doc Brown) invented a device he called "the flux capacitor," which he attached to the engine of a DeLorean automobile. The car had to reach a speed of eighty-eight miles per hour, at which point the flux capacitor was activated and the car would reach a velocity achieving time travel, taking its passengers back to the date selected on the dashboard of the car.

The flux capacitor had one major challenge. It took 1.21 jigawatts of electrical power to make it work. The only thing known to power it was the kind of impossible-to-acquire uranium required to generate nuclear power. So that's the setup to today's thought.

Remember Saturday's question: What are we?

Remember the answer: We are an extraordinarily unusual type of created being made by God to be a phylum beneath the order of angelic beings, possessing incomprehensible capacities and remarkable potential. We are made in the very image of the God of heaven and earth.

Bringing it all together now, this is why I went on Amazon and ordered a flux capacitor: At the core of who and what we are is a flux capacitor. The Bible, of course, doesn't call it this. The Bible calls it the "inmost being." Note how the Bible speaks of it:

For you created my inmost being;
you knit me together in my mother's womb.
I praise you because I am fearfully and wonderfully made;
your works are wonderful,
I know that full well.

Now watch how it works:

> I pray that out of his glorious riches he may strengthen you with power through his Spirit in your inner being, so that Christ may dwell in your hearts through faith. And I pray that you, being rooted and established in love, may have power, together with all the Lord's holy people, to grasp how wide and long and high and deep is the love of Christ, and to know this love that surpasses knowledge—that you may be filled to the measure of all the fullness of God. (Eph. 3:16–19)

Are you seeing it yet? Say it with me now, this time with conviction:

I am an unbelievable, inconceivable, unrepeatable miracle of God!

PRAY

Our Father, thank you for your Son, Jesus. Lord Jesus, we praise you because we are fearfully and wonderfully made. In your image we are unbelievable, inconceivable, unrepeatable miracles of God. Come, Holy Spirit, and lead us into the fullness of life in your image, in your name, amen.

JOURNAL

So, what do you make of this flux capacitor concept? What powers the flux capacitor of the inmost being? (Hint: The third person of the Trinity.)

Tuesday, Day 24

The Power of Transformational Questions

CONSECRATE

Wake up, sleeper, rise from the dead,
and Christ will shine on you. (Eph. 5:14)

Jesus, I belong to you.
I lift up my heart to you.
I set my mind on you.
I fix my eyes on you.
I offer my body to you as a living sacrifice.
Jesus, we belong to you.
Praying in the name of the Father and of the Son and of the Holy Spirit, amen.

READ

Mark 12:28–31

One of the teachers of the law came and heard them debating. Noticing that Jesus had given them a good answer, he asked him, "Of all the commandments, which is the most important?"

"The most important one," answered Jesus, "is this: 'Hear, O Israel: The Lord our God, the Lord is one. Love the Lord your God with all your heart and with all your soul and with all your mind and with all your strength.' The second is this: 'Love your neighbor as yourself.' There is no commandment greater than these."

CONSIDER

There is nothing quite so powerful as a well-asked question. The ancient philosopher Socrates is credited with the saying "Understanding a question is half the answer." Interestingly, he is also credited with saying, "The only true wisdom is in knowing you know nothing." His celebrated Socratic method, an approach to learning built around questions, continues to the present day as a treasured approach to education. Unfortunately, most of us have been trained in an educational system and model which prizes knowing the right answers. We are taught from an early age to seek the answers. It took me many years beyond my formal education to learn how to seek the questions.

It turns out Jesus was quite fond of questions. A quick search of the Bible reveals Jesus asked some 307 questions. They range from questions like "Do you want to get well?" to "What do you want me to do for you?" to the question of all questions: "But what about you? Who do you say that I am?"

He was asked 183 questions by others, questions like "Why don't your disciples fast?" and "What is the greatest commandment?"

Interestingly, of all those questions, he directly answered only three of them.

I will always remember an early conversation with my chief mentor, Maxie Dunnam, who has walked with me for more than thirty years as of this writing. As we sat across the table over coffee, he said, "John David, you will never outgrow the depth of the questions you are willing to consistently ask yourself."

When it comes to God and faith and the Bible, everyone has a plethora of questions, and most people like to take a crack at opining an answer to those of others. Fewer people ask themselves challenging questions, and even fewer do so consistently.

Maxie then told me there were three questions he had consistently asked himself over the course of many years. Of course, you know what my next question to him was:

"Would you teach me those three questions?"

And now I sense you are asking the same of me.

Over the next few days, I will share with you the three transformational questions I learned from my mentor and have asked myself for many years now.

In the meantime, I have a couple of questions for you.

Are there any questions you have consistently asked yourself over the years? If so, what might those questions be? If not, what might be a question or two you could start asking yourself about your life and discipleship to Jesus?

PRAY

Our Father, thank you for your Son, Jesus. Lord Jesus, we confess we are more about the answers than the questions. Train us in the art of asking transformational questions. By your Spirit, we are open and ready, even curious. What will you ask us? Praying in Jesus's name, amen.

JOURNAL

Any questions? Want to take a guess at what the three questions might be? It will be fun.

Wednesday, Day 25

Transformational Question 1

CONSECRATE

Wake up, sleeper, rise from the dead,
and Christ will shine on you. (Eph. 5:14)

Jesus, I belong to you.
I lift up my heart to you.
I set my mind on you.
I fix my eyes on you.
I offer my body to you as a living sacrifice.
Jesus, we belong to you.
Praying in the name of the Father and of the Son and of the Holy Spirit, amen.

READ

2 Peter 3:18

But grow in the grace and knowledge of our Lord and Savior Jesus Christ. To him be glory both now and forever! Amen.

CONSIDER

Everyone talks about Jesus as the answer. What if Jesus is actually more interested in being the question? After all, over the course of his life and work, he asked more than 300 questions (that we have written down). He was asked 183 questions by others. He directly answered only three of them.

Simply working through that body of questions would make a fascinating master class.

Here's a small sample of three from two chapters in Matthew's gospel:

If you love those who love you, what reward will you get? (5:46a)

If you greet only your brothers, what more are you doing than others? (5:47 ESV)

Can any one of you by worrying add a single hour to your life? (6:27)

The question Jesus asked the most, coming in at seven times, began with these words: "Have you never/not read . . . ?" Wow! Think maybe we should read more?

So back to the three transformational questions of my mentor, Maxie. In Mr. Miyagi fashion, he spoke these piercing words straight into my soul: "John David, you will never outgrow the depth of the questions you are willing to consistently ask yourself." Next, he raised three fingers as he said, "I want you to begin regularly asking yourself these three questions. The first question is this one: Am I growing?"

Before he could get to the second question, I immediately launched into answering the first one. I began to recount for Maxie the various ways I was reading the Bible and what I was gaining from the practice. Then I talked about my prayer life and how I knew I needed to be praying more and growing in my practice of fasting. Then I remembered how I had been trying to keep the Sabbath in a more regular way, and I started to humblebrag about that too.

Maxie kindly interrupted me. "The question was not about your devotional activities and spiritual practices. The question is: 'Am I growing?'"

Then it hit me. My growth in faith is not measured by my activities but by the transforming work of God in and through my life. The question is not, What am I doing? but What is God doing?

Am I growing?

How would I know? If the marks of my growth couldn't be measured by my activities—good and spiritual as they might be—how might growth be assessed?

Isn't it something how a good question rarely leads to a quick answer but rather to more good questions?

Bottom line: Religious activity is not the measure of transformational growth.

So what is? I want you to grapple with this question today. What is the measure of transformational growth? Then I want you to ask yourself the first transformational question: Am I growing?

PRAY

Lord Jesus, we want to start by asking you, "Am I growing?" You know us better than we know ourselves. What do you have to say about this question? How would you have us reflect on it? Please guide us. Praying in your name, amen.

JOURNAL

So, asking again, what is the measure of transformational growth?

Thursday, Day 26

On the Difference Between Winners and Losers

CONSECRATE

Wake up, sleeper, rise from the dead,
and Christ will shine on you. (Eph. 5:14)

Jesus, I belong to you.
I lift up my heart to you.
I set my mind on you.
I fix my eyes on you.
I offer my body to you as a living sacrifice.
Jesus, we belong to you.
Praying in the name of the Father and of the Son and of
the Holy Spirit, amen.

READ

2 Peter 1:5–8

For this very reason, make every effort to add to your faith goodness; and to goodness, knowledge; and to knowledge, self-control; and to self-control, perseverance; and to perseverance, godliness; and to godliness, mutual affection; and to mutual affection, love. For if you possess these qualities in increasing measure, they will keep you from being ineffective and unproductive in your knowledge of our Lord Jesus Christ.

CONSIDER

You know me, I immediately pressed Maxie for the second and third transformational questions. Again, in Mr. Miyagi fashion, he repeated the controlling concern: "John David, you will never outgrow the depth of the questions you are willing to consistently ask yourself." Then he added to the doctrine, "These are not questions you learn to master. They are questions you must allow to master you. You must let these questions penetrate to your depths."

Then he pressed, "So, are you growing?"

I replied, "Well, yes, and at the same time I'm not sure yet."

As I reflected more deeply on the question, I remembered a report I had given to our board of directors at Seedbed. In it, I offered growth statistic after growth statistic of how many people had visited our website and how many people had downloaded different free resources and how many people had purchased a book, and I talked about the incredible margins of growth. (I should add, it's easy to show high-percentage data points of so-called growth in a new company because it started at zero.)

The deeper truth underneath all those so-called growth measures (a.k.a. vanity metrics) was that our company had plateaued and was not really growing at all. I stopped myself mid-sentence in the report and asked the board this transformational question:

"Do you all know who focuses on statistics?" Answering my own question, I replied: "Losers." I followed up with another transformational question: "Do you know what winners focus on?" Again, I answered: "The score." Then I added, in a confessional tone, "I'm not sure we know what the score is or even what the scorecard looks like."

What's true for organizations is doubly true for a person. When you don't know the score, it is easy to report on statistics. In other words, when you can't prove transformational growth, it's tempting to report on how much you have been going to church. When you aren't sure if you are growing, it's a seductive sleight of hand to try to prove you've been busy.

My first real growth metric was to actually develop a growth metric—a real scorecard—and to stop measuring mere activity. I'll say more about that scorecard later. In the meantime, here is some food for thought:

For this very reason, make every effort to add to your faith goodness; and to goodness, knowledge; and to knowledge, self-control; and to self-control, perseverance; and to perseverance, godliness; and to godliness, mutual affection; and to mutual affection, love. For if you possess these qualities in increasing measure, they will keep you from being ineffective and unproductive in your knowledge of our Lord Jesus Christ.

Let me ask you: What do you think are the markers or metrics of real transformational growth? After all, how can you answer Transformational Question 1, "Am I growing?," if you don't know how or in what measure you are attempting to grow? So, what might our scorecard look like?

PRAY

Our Father, thank you for your Son, Jesus. Lord Jesus, something tells us you are the measure of transformational growth. But how on earth might we begin to measure this? Save us from the trap of becoming negative about ourselves and lead us into the solution of becoming super positive about you. Praying in your name, amen.

JOURNAL

What do you think are the markers or metrics of real transformational growth?

Friday, Day 27

Growth Is a Game of Degrees and Inches

CONSECRATE

Wake up, sleeper, rise from the dead,
and Christ will shine on you. (Eph. 5:14)

Jesus, I belong to you.
I lift up my heart to you.
I set my mind on you.
I fix my eyes on you.
I offer my body to you as a living sacrifice.
Jesus, we belong to you.
Praying in the name of the Father and of the Son and of the Holy Spirit, amen.

READ

2 Corinthians 3:18 ESV

And we all, with unveiled face, beholding the glory of the Lord, are being transformed into the same image from one degree of glory to another. For this comes from the Lord who is the Spirit.

CONSIDER

Between my two sisters and me we have eight children: four from me and two each from them. We love it when we can all be together at my parents' home. We call it "Cousin Camp." One of the steadfast rituals over their growing-up years was the practice the cousins call "measuring." In my parents' home, the chimney from the downstairs fireplace is fully exposed in the upstairs great room. On each side of each corner of the chimney is a series of marks with measurements written next to them. There are eight measuring rods, one for each cousin.

One by one they backed up to their particular measuring rod, and someone (usually me) put a ruler next to their head and marked their current height. The measuring was not a contest against each other to see who was the tallest but a way for each one to assess how much they had grown since the last measurement. Everyone was always so eager to see how much they had grown.

It brings the first transformational question into sharp focus, doesn't it?

Am I growing?

I wonder what measuring might look like when it comes to growing in our faith and maturing in our Christlike character.

The fascinating thing about both physical and spiritual growth is how slowly it actually happens and yet, at the same time, how dramatic it can be over lengthy intervals of time. From year to year the growth of any given cousin is pretty small, but over a five-year period, the growth can be quite dramatic. Our physical bodies grow by inches. The Bible indicates our souls grow by degrees:

And we all, with unveiled face, beholding the glory of the Lord, are being transformed into the same image from one degree of glory to another. For this comes from the Lord who is the Spirit.

What does one degree of glory look like? How might we attempt to measure it? I can already hear the objections. "Growth in the grace of God can't be measured." We live in an age where everything in the universe—from white blood cells to light-years—can be and, in fact, is measured. Surely we can find a meaningful way to measure transformational growth. The real question is: Do we have the will to measure it?

PRAY

Our Father, thank you for your Son, Jesus. Lord Jesus, you are the glory of God and every degree of it. By your Spirit, would you begin to reveal to us what growing by one degree of glory could look like in ordinary people like us? And beyond that, how might such growth happen? Praying in your name, amen.

JOURNAL

Will you grapple with this matter today? We will dive in deeper tomorrow, but I wonder how you might define a degree of glory and how you might go about measuring it.

Saturday, Day 28

Staying Out of the Performance-Evaluation Ditch

CONSECRATE

Wake up, sleeper, rise from the dead,
and Christ will shine on you. (Eph. 5:14)

Jesus, I belong to you.
I lift up my heart to you.
I set my mind on you.
I fix my eyes on you.
I offer my body to you as a living sacrifice.
Jesus, we belong to you.
Praying in the name of the Father and of the Son and of the Holy Spirit, amen.

READ

Ephesians 4:22–24

You were taught, with regard to your former way of life, to put off your old self, which is being corrupted by its deceitful desires; to be made new in the attitude of your minds; and to put on the new self, created to be like God in true righteousness and holiness.

CONSIDER

Do you remember your last performance evaluation? Sometimes employers call them "annual reviews" to soften the edge. They rank right up there with wisdom teeth removal and cleaning out the refrigerator for most of us. We work hard, do our best, show up early, stay late, and answer emails on the weekend. Then, like clockwork, every year the dreaded day comes when we sit awkwardly across the desk from our boss or supervisor. We receive a few obligatory affirmations and recognitions and then comes the list of places where we didn't quite measure up and the things we need to improve. No matter how great the accolades were, we walk away hyperfocused on (and often defensive about) our shortcomings.

I think this is why we shy away from the whole notion of measuring transformation. We think of it as a divine performance evaluation. We know we missed the mark and dropped a lot of balls, and we would rather just not go there and push the "God loves us anyway" button.

This is a tricky path we are walking now. Maybe that's why Jesus said it was a narrow way and that few find it (see Matt. 7:14). But what if few actually find it because they perceive it as too narrow and they just don't want to go there? Okay, one more question: Could it be that we fundamentally misunderstand the whole process and dynamic of transformation?

You were taught, with regard to your former way of life, to put off your old self, which is being corrupted by its deceitful desires; to be made new in the attitude of your minds; and to put on the new self, created to be like God in true righteousness and holiness.

Measuring degrees of glory is not a performance evaluation but a transformation review. Now, what if I told you that you are not the performer, the one being evaluated? Measuring degrees of glory is a review of the transformational work of Jesus in you. This is not about where you have measured up or missed the mark. It is about how Jesus has transformed you from one degree of glory to the next. I repeat, this is not your spiritual performance evaluation. It is an assessment and analysis of Jesus's transformational process in you.

Translation: The pressure is off. The power is on.

PRAY

Our Father, thank you for your Son, Jesus. Lord Jesus, you don't just bring the transformation; you are the transformation. What a relief. We don't need to perform. We do need to learn more about how to yield to your presence in us—the new self, created to be like God in true righteousness and holiness. That's what we want. Come, Holy Spirit, and make it so. Praying in Jesus's name, amen.

JOURNAL

Are you ready for the new self—the one created to be like God? How about the new way of receiving the new self as opposed to the old way of trying harder to be better and do more?

Fifth Sunday of Lent

That same day Jesus went out of the house and sat by the lake. Such large crowds gathered around him that he got into a boat and sat in it, while all the people stood on the shore. Then he told them many things in parables, saying: "A farmer went out to sow his seed. As he was scattering the seed, some fell along the path, and the birds came and ate it up. Some fell on rocky places, where it did not have much soil. It sprang up quickly, because the soil was shallow. But when the sun came up, the plants were scorched, and they withered because they had no root. Other seed fell among thorns, which grew up and choked the plants. Still other seed fell on good soil, where it produced a crop—a hundred, sixty or thirty times what was sown. Whoever has ears, let them hear." . . .

"Listen then to what the parable of the sower means: When anyone hears the message about the kingdom and does not understand it, the evil one comes and snatches away what was sown in their heart. This is the seed sown along the path. The seed falling on rocky ground refers to someone who hears the word and at once receives it with joy. But since they have no root, they last only a short time. When trouble or persecution comes because of the word, they quickly fall away. The seed falling among the thorns refers to someone who hears the word, but the worries of this life and the deceitfulness of wealth choke the word, making it unfruitful. But the seed falling on good soil refers to someone who hears the word and understands it. This is the one who produces a crop, yielding a hundred, sixty or thirty times what was sown."

—Matthew 13:1–9, 18–23

Monday, Day 29

From Self-Improvement to Real Transformation

CONSECRATE

Wake up, sleeper, rise from the dead,
and Christ will shine on you. (Eph. 5:14)

Jesus, I belong to you.
I lift up my heart to you.
I set my mind on you.
I fix my eyes on you.
I offer my body to you as a living sacrifice.
Jesus, we belong to you.
Praying in the name of the Father and of the Son and of the Holy Spirit, amen.

READ

Philippians 1:3–6

I thank my God every time I remember you. In all my prayers for all of you, I always pray with joy because of your partnership in the gospel from the first day until now, being confident of this, that he who began a good work in you will carry it on to completion until the day of Christ Jesus.

CONSIDER

Can you believe we are still on Transformational Question 1?

Am I growing?

It turns out the answer to this question is actually the more important question: "How is Jesus transforming me?"

We must constantly be reminded of this fact. Transformation is not self-improvement. Remember our watchword from Transfiguration Mountain? *Metamorphoō.* It means transcendent formation. It is a change process coming from outside of us to the deep inmost place inside of us, coming from somewhere else—indeed, from Someone else—and working from the inside out. Transformation shows up in our outside self, but it begins deep on the inside.

He who began a good work in you . . .

Transformation originates with Jesus.

. . . will carry it on to completion until the day of Christ Jesus.

Transformation continues, is carried forward, and completed by Jesus.

Yes, the secret to transformation is Jesus himself.

Did I tell you the story of how I first met Maxie, my mentor? I was his yardman. Yes, I mowed the yard and raked the leaves and pruned the trees and cultivated the roses and peonies and hydrangeas, and I could go on. It was my first year of seminary at Asbury Theological Seminary in Wilmore, Kentucky. Maxie was the new president. I had been hired to keep the grounds—forty acres—where he and his wife, Jerry, lived.

One morning, I was there early and needed to ask him something. As I opened the back door, I could hear him talking. *Wait*, I thought to myself. *Is he talking to himself?* Someone was shouting his name, and it sounded like his own distinctive voice. Here's what he was saying: "Maxie, the secret is simply this: Christ in you! Yes, Christ in you bringing with him the hope of all glorious things to come."

When I asked him about it, he said it was his adaptation of the J. B. Phillips translation of Colossians 1:27. Maxie said he began every day by declaring this Word of God aloud over himself.

Yes, the secret to transformation is Jesus himself.

Self-improvement puts self in the driver's seat. It rides on the rails of the ten two-letter words: If it is to be, it is up to me. Self-improvement will gladly ask Jesus for assistance, but Jesus doesn't do self-improvement. He traffics in transformation.

He is the beginning, the middle, and the end of transformation. The secret is inviting him to sit enthroned over your life and ceding all control over to him.

I've tried to follow Maxie in his approach to following Jesus. Would you join me?

"[Insert your name here], the secret is simply this: Christ in you! Yes, Christ in you bringing with him the hope of all glorious things to come."

Write that in your journal today.

PRAY

Our Father, thank you for your Son, Jesus. Lord Jesus, you are the secret of transformation because you are the transformation yourself. Transform our minds with this fact until our minds are finally renewed. By the Holy Spirit, we cede all control to you. Our temples are henceforth under new management. Praying in your name, amen.

JOURNAL

Is it registering with you yet that you are not doing the transformation in your own life? How about this amended phrase: "If it is to be, it is up to Jesus in me"? What are the implications of this amendment?

Tuesday, Day 30

You Had One Job . . .

CONSECRATE

Wake up, sleeper, rise from the dead,
and Christ will shine on you. (Eph. 5:14)

Jesus, I belong to you.
I lift up my heart to you.
I set my mind on you.
I fix my eyes on you.
I offer my body to you as a living sacrifice.
Jesus, we belong to you.
Praying in the name of the Father and of the Son and of the Holy Spirit, amen.

READ

1 Corinthians 3:6
I planted the seed, Apollos watered it, but God has been making it grow.

CONSIDER

The Bible is decisively growth oriented when it comes to our faith and maturity in the character of Jesus. Every book, every letter, every story in one way or another is about growing in the likeness of Jesus Christ. The whole storyline of the Bible might be summarized as the story of creation to new creation. The Bible started in a garden of trees and rivers, and it will end with a river lined by trees whose leaves are for the healing of the nations.

I planted the seed, Apollos watered it, but God has been making it grow.

But it is so critical that we grasp who does what in this process. We do not make things grow. We cannot make ourselves grow. Jesus, ever trying to open our eyes to how his kingdom works, put it like this:

> He also said, "This is what the kingdom of God is like. A man scatters seed on the ground. Night and day, whether he sleeps or gets up, the seed sprouts and grows, though he does not know how. All by itself the soil produces grain—first

> the stalk, then the head, then the full kernel in the head. As soon as the grain is ripe, he puts the sickle to it, because the harvest has come." (Mark 4:26–29)

I planted the seed, Apollos watered it, but God has been making it grow.

It is settled. God makes it grow. Pressure's off. But did you catch the part we play?

I planted the seed.

A person scatters seed on the ground.

We plant the seed. But what is the seed? In his celebrated parable of the sower, Jesus made it clear: "The seed is the word of God" (Luke 8:11).

Our part is to plant the Word of God in the soil of our lives. How do we do this? There's a lot to be said on this point, but this comes to mind. Remember Maxie's daily affirmation? Every day he plants the seed of this Word of God in the soil of his life:

"Maxie, the secret is simply this: Christ in you! Yes, Christ in you bringing with him the hope of all glorious things to come" (adapted from Col. 1:27 Phillips).

I wonder, what Word of God are you planting in the soil of your life these days? What seeds of Scripture are you scattering across the field of your soul? Our job is to plant the seed of God's Word in our lives—every single day.

Here's what we don't want to hear Jesus one day say to us: "You had one job . . ."

Here's what I know: Whatever Word you are planting, that Word is prospering. It is growing the very goodness of God in your soul.

PRAY

Our Father, thank you for your Son, Jesus. Lord Jesus, thank you for the seed of the Word of God, and thank you that you yourself are the Word of God made flesh, the picture of what happens when the Word of God is realized in a human being by the power of the Holy Spirit. Let the Word become enfleshed in our lives by the same Spirit. Praying in your name, amen.

JOURNAL

Have you ever considered that no matter how technologically advanced the world gets, it still can't make a seed grow? The soil matters, but the secret is in the seed. How does this increase your confidence in the Word of God?

Wednesday, Day 31

The Most Excellent Way to Measure What Matters Most

CONSECRATE

Wake up, sleeper, rise from the dead,
and Christ will shine on you. (Eph. 5:14)

Jesus, I belong to you.
I lift up my heart to you.
I set my mind on you.
I fix my eyes on you.
I offer my body to you as a living sacrifice.
Jesus, we belong to you.
Praying in the name of the Father and of the Son and of the Holy Spirit, amen.

READ

1 Corinthians 13:1–3

If I speak in the tongues of men or of angels, but do not have love, I am only a resounding gong or a clanging cymbal. If I have the gift of prophecy and can fathom all mysteries and all knowledge, and if I have a faith that can move mountains, but do not have love, I am nothing. If I give all I possess to the poor and give over my body to hardship that I may boast, but do not have love, I gain nothing.

CONSIDER

A few years back, one of my friends, Nick, who is also a colleague on the Farm Team (staff) at Seedbed, and I embarked on an experiment. We shared a keen interest in growing in our experience and expression of the love of God. We also felt stuck in that process. We were in a discipleship band together, which was helping, but we knew we were missing something. We wanted to grow in love, but other than a touchy-feely subjective sense of how we were doing, we didn't know how to measure our growth. Then we had a BFO—a blinding flash of the obvious.

The Bible has a remarkable set of measurements when it comes to love. It can be found in the thirteenth chapter of Paul's first letter to the Corinthians. It has been called "the Love Chapter" and "the Wedding Text," which is perhaps why we had never considered it before. Nick and I agreed together that we would "rememberize" this text and make it a point of our ongoing conversation for the rest of our lives. (For those who aren't yet aware, "rememberize" is different from "memorize." To memorize is the quick loading of the short term memory; to rememberize is the slow loading of the long term memory.)

The chapter opens with a truly remarkable set of observations. It lists all the attributes of a highly successful Christian. I'll break them down here:

1. Being supernaturally gifted with foreign languages without having studied them in order to proclaim the gospel of the kingdom of Jesus to people who do not yet know him
2. Being supernaturally gifted with an angelic language in order to communicate with God through prayer in extraordinary expressions
3. Possessing the supernatural ability to convey divine communication from God to other people for their care and benefit
4. Possessing the supernatural ability to discern and understand wisdom and mysteries and knowledge about seemingly unknowable things
5. Being filled with the supernatural gift of faith to such an extent one has the capacity to do impossible things (i.e., move mountains)

6. Being possessed of a supernatural generosity so extravagant that one gives away all they own to the poor
7. Being possessed of a supernatural gift of courage so profound that one gives up their body to the death of a martyr for the glory of God

What the Bible says next in this celebrated text is truly remarkable. It says if a person does all these heroic and saintly things and yet lacks one thing, then all of it has been worthless, a complete failure and waste of time. In other words, all these amazing things are not the measure of transformational growth. So what is the missing measure in the eternal equation?

Love.

Yes, love. It is explicitly mentioned or referenced twenty-one times in the thirteen verses of this chapter.

Love is the measure.

Though it may be expressed in myriad manifestations, the transformational answer to the first transformational question comes down to one measurement.

Love.

PRAY

Our Father, thank you for your Son, Jesus. Lord Jesus, you are the definition of love. And you love because you are love. And you are the secret in me that makes me love. Come, Holy Spirit, and empower me to live in and from this love. Praying in your name, amen.

JOURNAL

Do you think of love as soft and fuzzy and not really the main thing? Or has it hit you that love is hardcore and the whole thing? How does what you think about love measure up to how the Bible actually talks about love?

Thursday, Day 32

The Measuring Stick of Transformational Growth

CONSECRATE

Wake up, sleeper, rise from the dead,
and Christ will shine on you. (Eph. 5:14)

Jesus, I belong to you.
I lift up my heart to you.
I set my mind on you.
I fix my eyes on you.
I offer my body to you as a living sacrifice.
Jesus, we belong to you.
Praying in the name of the Father and of the Son and of the Holy Spirit, amen.

READ

1 Corinthians 13:4–8a

Love is patient, love is kind. It does not envy, it does not boast, it is not proud. It does not dishonor others, it is not self-seeking, it is not easily angered, it keeps no record of wrongs. Love does not delight in evil but rejoices with the truth. It always protects, always trusts, always hopes, always perseveres.

Love never fails.

CONSIDER

Though it is unclear exactly what the Beatles meant when they said that all we need is love, they were exactly right.

And to be sure, definitions matter, for *love* has come to mean so many things that it means nothing definitively at all. We must peer behind the translated English word *love* to see the word chosen for our text in the original Greek language.

The Greek word hiding behind the translated English word *love*, appearing or referenced some twenty-one times in this chapter of only thirteen verses, is *agape*.

It means, in short, divine love. We are talking about the love of God.

Back to the question: Are you growing? My impulse was to measure myself against this marker of divine love. So I created a measuring stick of sorts. First, I took the text and inserted a blank everywhere the word *love* was written or referenced.

_______ is patient, _______ is kind. _______ does not envy, _______ does not boast, _______ is not proud. _______ does not dishonor others, _______ is not self-seeking, _______ is not easily angered, _______ keeps no record of wrongs. _______ does not delight in evil but _______ rejoices with the truth. _______ always protects, _______ always trusts, _______ always hopes, _______ always perseveres. _______ never fails.

Second, I wrote my name in each of the blanks, and then I read the paragraph aloud to see if I could pass the straight-face test. Then it hit me. I was doing it all wrong. I was attempting to measure my performance against a divine standard. The Christian life is not about my performance, but Jesus's power. So I added another step.

In each of the blanks I had made, I entered another name. Any guesses as to whose name?

Jesus is patient, Jesus is kind. Jesus does not envy, Jesus does not boast, Jesus is not proud. Jesus does not dishonor others, Jesus is not self-seeking, Jesus is not easily angered, Jesus keeps no record of wrongs. Jesus does not delight in evil but Jesus rejoices with the truth. Jesus always protects, Jesus always trusts, Jesus always hopes, Jesus always perseveres. Jesus never fails.

Now cue our adapted declaration of Colossians 1:27: "[Insert your name here], the secret is simply this: Christ in you! Yes, Christ in you, bringing with him the hope of all glorious things to come."

If Jesus is agape love and Jesus is in me, I am agape love. Jesus is the performer. I am the participant. He is the revelation. I am the responder. My life now becomes a studied participation in his life, an empowered improvisation of his craft, an infused reception and profuse demonstration of his love.

PRAY

Our Father, thank you for your Son, Jesus. Lord Jesus, your life is the vision of love. We want to behold this vision, in broad expanse and super up close—how wide and how high and how deep and how long. We want to become this kind of love. Come, Holy Spirit, and reveal and unveil it in and through us. Praying in Jesus's name, amen.

JOURNAL

Can you remember a Jesus story for each of the dynamics of love listed in 1 Corinthians 13? Can you find one?

Friday, Day 33

Transformational Question 2

CONSECRATE

Wake up, sleeper, rise from the dead,
and Christ will shine on you. (Eph. 5:14)

Jesus, I belong to you.
I lift up my heart to you.
I set my mind on you.
I fix my eyes on you.
I offer my body to you as a living sacrifice.
Jesus, we belong to you.
Praying in the name of the Father and of the Son and of the Holy Spirit, amen.

READ

2 Peter 1:3–4
His divine power has given us everything we need for a godly life through our knowledge of him who called us by his own glory and goodness. Through these he has given us his very great and precious promises, so that through them you may participate in the divine nature, having escaped the corruption in the world caused by evil desires.

CONSIDER

He held up two fingers. The day had finally come. I was not graduating from Transformational Question 1, but I would finally learn Transformational Question 2. My mentor, Maxie, sat across the table from me with two fingers raised. We rehearsed the first question: Am I growing?

He reminded me that the question was not addressed from him to me, as in, "Are you growing?" Rather, he said you must come to the place where you are willing to genuinely and persistently ask the question of yourself, "Am I growing?"

We remembered also that our growing does not come as a product of our efforts but as a result of God's initiative—Christ in you bringing with him all the glorious things. Then he shared this text to emphasize his point:

His divine power has given us everything we need for a godly life through our knowledge of him who called us by his own glory and goodness.

And then with all the seasoned drama of a Desert Father, he offered the second question: Do I really want to change?

Again, it is me asking myself—not someone else asking me. Two, nay, three key words here. Notice the word *really*. It leads us past the water table of interest and into the deep well of intention. Notice the second key word: *want*. I may think I need to change. In fact, I may know I need to change, but thinking and knowing and needing are not part of the question at all.

Do I really want to change?

Remember, I am not asking you the question. I am asking you to ask yourself the question. It will hit deeper if you ask the question aloud.

Do I really want to change?

The third key word? *Change*. It brings us back to where we started—the Mount of Transfiguration. Remember the watchword, the original word behind the English word *transfiguration*? *Metamorphoō*. It means transformation, or transcendent formation, which is the very presence of God entering into the form of a human being—the temple of the human body—and bringing the change. In perhaps one of the most stunning texts in all Scripture, Peter writes about the story of transformation, of *metamorphoō*, and, yes, of change.

Through these he has given us his very great and precious promises, so that through them you may participate in the divine nature, having escaped the corruption in the world caused by evil desires.

Now back to that day with Maxie. Rather than launch into my answer to Transformational Question 2, I asked him another question: "So what is the change you are talking about?"

With the slightest tone of irritation, he replied, "Stick with the question."

Do I really want to change?

PRAY

Our Father, thank you for your Son, Jesus. Lord Jesus, you are the change. We are weary of trying harder to change our nature. We want to participate in your nature. Come, Holy Spirit, and bring us the change who is Jesus. Praying in your name, amen.

JOURNAL

What do you think it means to participate in the divine nature? What scares you about change?

Saturday, Day 34

What Is This Change and How Do I Participate?

CONSECRATE

Wake up, sleeper, rise from the dead,
and Christ will shine on you. (Eph. 5:14)

Jesus, I belong to you.
I lift up my heart to you.
I set my mind on you.
I fix my eyes on you.
I offer my body to you as a living sacrifice.
Jesus, we belong to you.
Praying in the name of the Father and of the Son and of the Holy Spirit, amen.

READ

John 5:1–6

Some time later, Jesus went up to Jerusalem for one of the Jewish festivals. Now there is in Jerusalem near the Sheep Gate a pool, which in Aramaic is called Bethesda and which is surrounded by five covered colonnades. Here a great number of disabled people used to lie—the blind, the lame, the paralyzed. One who was there had been an invalid for thirty-eight years. When Jesus saw him lying there and learned that he had been in this condition for a long time, he asked him, "Do you want to get well?"

CONSIDER

Transformational Question 2 is now in play:

Do I really want to change?

It reminds me of that day with Jesus at the Pool of Siloam. You read the story. The man had been out of commission for thirty-eight years—lost to his life, languishing, and hopeless. But he was there that day, and one gets the sense he had been there for many days before. Can we just surmise his answer to Transformational Question 1, "Am I growing?," was a resounding no? Notice how Jesus goes straight for Transformational Question 2:

"Do you want to get well?"

Something tells me no one had ever asked him this question. I'm sure people had told him to own his life or to get a job or to take his medicine or to lose weight and a hundred other helpful pro tips that never work. With six piercing words Jesus cut through the layers of disability and diagnosed the deeper sickness—his abdication of responsibility.

Look at his answer:

"Sir," the invalid replied, "I have no one to help me into the pool when the water is stirred. While I am trying to get in, someone else goes down ahead of me" (v. 7).

He had his reasons. We all do. Our seeming intractable situations and conditions are usually someone else's fault, right? Even so, we retain responsibility, which is another way of saying the ability to respond. What we need is what Jesus brings—revelation. Indeed, it is who he is. We need to encounter him face-to-face, heart-to-heart, and hear his question to us:

"Do you want to get well?"

When we hear this revealed question from Jesus, we must ask ourselves the deeper question: Do I really want to change?

This question cuts through all the tired emotional eddies of our inner brokenness, pierces the veil of our latent victimhood, and repairs the damaged nerve of our reluctance to repent. Jesus knows the issue is at the level of our will. He wants access to our volition.

Do I really want to change?

And we haven't even talked about what the change is yet. This question goes deeper than that. It is about recovering our response-ability. This is the crucible question where we begin the transformational exchange of our will for the good, pleasing, and perfect will of God (see Rom. 12:2).

PRAY

Our Father, thank you for your Son, Jesus. Lord Jesus, we know we need to change, but that isn't the question. We are not certain we really want to change. We can honestly say we want to want to change. Thank you for accepting us as we are and not as we think we should be. Come, Holy Spirit, and deepen our desire to change. Praying in Jesus's name, amen.

JOURNAL

How do you reflect on these three words: *really*, *want*, *change*? When is the last time you asked yourself what you really want?

Sixth Sunday of Lent

As they approached Jerusalem and came to Bethphage on the Mount of Olives, Jesus sent two disciples, saying to them, "Go to the village ahead of you, and at once you will find a donkey tied there, with her colt by her. Untie them and bring them to me. If anyone says anything to you, say that the Lord needs them, and he will send them right away."

This took place to fulfill what was spoken through the prophet:

> "Say to Daughter Zion,
> 'See, your king comes to you,
> gentle and riding on a donkey,
> and on a colt, the foal of a donkey.'"

The disciples went and did as Jesus had instructed them. They brought the donkey and the colt and placed their cloaks on them for Jesus to sit on. A very large crowd spread their cloaks on the road, while others cut branches from the trees and spread them on the road. The crowds that went ahead of him and those that followed shouted,

"Hosanna to the Son of David!"

"Blessed is he who comes in the name of the Lord!"

"Hosanna in the highest heaven!"

When Jesus entered Jerusalem, the whole city was stirred and asked, "Who is this?"

The crowds answered, "This is Jesus, the prophet from Nazareth in Galilee."

—Matthew 21:1–11

In your relationships with one another, have the same mindset as Christ Jesus:

Who, being in very nature God,
did not consider equality with God
something to be used to his own advantage;
rather, he made himself nothing
by taking the very nature of a servant,
being made in human likeness.
And being found in appearance as a man,
he humbled himself

by becoming obedient to death—
even death on a cross!
Therefore God exalted him to the highest place
and gave him the name that is above
every name,
that at the name of Jesus every knee should bow,
in heaven and on earth and under the earth,
and every tongue acknowledge that Jesus Christ
is Lord,
to the glory of God the Father.

—Philippians 2:5–11

Monday of Holy Week, Day 35

Why the Change Is an Exchange

CONSECRATE

Wake up, sleeper, rise from the dead,
and Christ will shine on you. (Eph. 5:14)

Jesus, I belong to you.
I lift up my heart to you.
I set my mind on you.
I fix my eyes on you.
I offer my body to you as a living sacrifice.
Jesus, we belong to you.
Praying in the name of the Father and of the Son and of the Holy Spirit, amen.

READ

Galatians 2:20

I have been crucified with Christ and I no longer live, but Christ lives in me. The life I now live in the body, I live by faith in the Son of God, who loved me and gave himself for me.

CONSIDER

Do I really want to change?

For the longest time I looked at the Christian faith and life as a kind of good-to-great program. I was a pretty good person with a lot of potential. I had some bad habits and a few flaws, but I had a good résumé and presented well. That's why, when Maxie asked me Transformational Question 2, my immediate response was to talk about all the ways I knew I needed to change, to go from good to great.

You remember what happened with Transformational Question 1—Am I growing? I launched into recounting all the spiritual activities in my rule of life. Maxie stopped me mid-sentence and said, "I didn't ask you about your spiritual activities list. I asked you to ask yourself if you were growing."

This time, after about five minutes of my self-righteous self-disclosure about all the changes I needed to make, he interrupted me again: "John David, I didn't ask if you felt you needed to change or even what changes you felt you needed to make. I asked you to ask yourself, 'Do I really want to change?'"And then he tracked out the core text of Transformational Question 2.

I have been crucified with Christ and I no longer live, but Christ lives in me. The life I now live in the body, I live by faith in the Son of God, who loved me and gave himself for me.

And that's when it hit me. There is capital-C Change and then there are the small-c changes.

The capital-C Change is Galatians 2:20. Ten words:

And I no longer live, but Christ lives in me.

It calls to mind those eleven ancient words we remembered on Transfiguration Mountain: "though the bush was on fire it did not burn up" (Ex. 3:2).

And then I started pulling all the threads.

The "me" in "but Christ lives in me" is the real me. It is the plan-A vision of me God had in mind when he imaged me in his image in the first place. It is the "unbelievable, inconceivable, unrepeatable miracle of God" version of me. It is the "why not be completely changed into fire" version of me. It is the "beholding as in a mirror the glory of the Lord and being transformed into the same image from one degree of glory to the next" version of me.

This is the change. Now, let me ask you to ask yourself the second transformational question I am asking myself: Do I really want to change?

PRAY

Our Father, thank you for your Son, Jesus. Lord Jesus, we want this change. We really want it—the change that is actually the exchange—our broken selves for your whole life, our sinfulness for your righteousness, our emptiness for your fullness. What we mean to say is we want you, Jesus. Praying in your name, amen.

JOURNAL

What in you resists really wanting this change? What do you imagine you would be like on the other side of this change?

Tuesday of Holy Week, Day 36

From My Old-Creation Self to My New-Creation Life

CONSECRATE

Wake up, sleeper, rise from the dead,
and Christ will shine on you. (Eph. 5:14)

Jesus, I belong to you.
I lift up my heart to you.
I set my mind on you.
I fix my eyes on you.
I offer my body to you as a living sacrifice.
Jesus, we belong to you.
Praying in the name of the Father and of the Son and of the Holy Spirit, amen.

READ

2 Corinthians 5:17 NASB

Therefore if anyone is in Christ, this person is a new creation; the old things passed away; behold, new things have come.

CONSIDER

Let's keep going with Transformational Question 2.

Do I really want to change?

Something tells me you answered that with a loud *yes* and a quiet *but*. Perhaps you are still lingering with yesterday's word and those ten words "And I no longer live but Christ lives in me" (Gal. 2:20).

The quiet *but* comes from a misunderstanding of those words "I no longer live." To say, "I no longer live," is not self-abnegation as some think. It means the old, fallen, broken, still-stuck-in-sin me no longer lives. To confess, "I no longer live," is not the loss of one's distinctive identity; rather, it is the declaration of the death of our false self.

To declare, "but Christ lives in me," is the movement toward our deepest and truest identity. I love how Paul puts it in another of his letters:

Therefore if anyone is in Christ, this person is a new creation; the old things passed away; behold, new things have come.

New-creation me is the person Jesus would be if Jesus were me. It is the mercy of his compassion displacing my lack of caring for people. It is the joy he carries even in sorrow displacing my despairing spirit. It is the generosity of his disposition displacing my scarcity mindset. It is everything we know and love about Jesus and his spacious personhood becoming true and realized through our unique personality.

It brings me to the next "Yes, but . . ." I can already hear you saying, "But I already believe all you are saying. I have really tried to change my old self and ways, but I'm still stuck in the same ruts. Yes, I love God, and I believe in Jesus, and I'm thankful for his death on the cross for me, but I've just not seen the kind of transformation you speak of, and I'm tired of trying so hard."

By the way, thanks for keeping it real. Because the old self dies slowly, our self-improvement mindset dies hard. The self-improvement mindset is me trying harder to do more to be better—in Jesus's name. It only produces a marginally better version of the old self.

New-creation me is not me trying harder but trusting deeply. It is not me changing myself with behavioral resolve. It is Jesus transforming me from within by divine presence. It is not me trying to make something happen.

It is me finally realizing and actually receiving what has, in fact, already happened. As the text says:

The old things passed away; behold, new things have come.

What if the reality is we've been doing it wrong? What if change happens not by resolve but by repentance? And what if repentance is not behavior modification (or worse, sin management) but realignment. What if it doesn't happen with a change of heart—which changes back all too easily—but by the renewal of the mind? Remember Romans 12:2, "Be transformed by the renewal of your mind."

The change that is transformation is brought on by the renewal of the mind, which leads to the renovation of the heart.

The capital-C Change and all the small-c changes do not come through behavior modification or sin management. Change starts with a mindset shift, which leads to the renewal of the mind. It is not believing and behaving. It is beholding and becoming. It is receiving and renewal.

PRAY

Our Father, thank you for your Son, Jesus. Lord Jesus, we really want our new-creation lives, which is another way of saying we really want to change. Forgive us for focusing on what is wrong with us. Train us to behold all that is right with you. Something tells us beholding you is the way to becoming like you. Praying in your name, amen.

JOURNAL

What do you make of this idea that the new-creation you is the person Jesus would be if Jesus were you? Can you describe that person, his life shining through your personhood and unique personality?

Wednesday of Holy Week, Day 37

Why I Am Not the Change Agent

CONSECRATE

Wake up, sleeper, rise from the dead,
and Christ will shine on you. (Eph. 5:14)

Jesus, I belong to you.
I lift up my heart to you.
I set my mind on you.
I fix my eyes on you.
I offer my body to you as a living sacrifice.
Jesus, we belong to you.
Praying in the name of the Father and of the Son and of the Holy Spirit, amen.

READ

John 15:1–2

I am the true vine, and my Father is the gardener. He cuts off every branch in me that bears no fruit, while every branch that does bear fruit he prunes so that it will be even more fruitful.

CONSIDER

The more I engage with Transformational Question 2, the more I find myself changing the question. Here's where I tend to go with it.

Do I really want to change . . . myself?

I am such a take-the-bull-by-the-horns, be-the-change, make-the-change kind of person. In other words, I am an activist. Full disclosure: I am or want to be a change agent. Jesus paints a different picture.

I am the true vine, and my Father is the gardener.

Here's my interpretation: "Put down the pruning shears. You are not the gardener. God is the gardener."

We plant the seed and we harvest the crop, but the journey from seed to seeds is the work and will of God. In his final hours with his disciples, Jesus labored to reveal this most critical truth about transformation. We are the planting of the Lord. He is the gardener. We are not the gardener. We participate by staying grounded, attached, and receptive.

He cuts off every branch in me that bears no fruit, while every branch that does bear fruit he prunes so that it will be even more fruitful.

The problem is we desperately want to be our own gardener and tend our own growth. This is bad religion. Even worse, we want to be the gardener of our neighbor's garden and tend their growth. This is bad religion on steroids. Down with bad religion. Up with good faith. That looks like John 15:3—"You are already clean because of the word I have spoken to you."

That word *clean* is closely related to the word *prune*. Jesus speaks the word, which prunes us. Our Father cuts the branches. So what is our part? How do we stay grounded, connected, and receptive? Jesus brings it down to a single word, and he repeats it over and over and over again. He says it four times in the fourth verse alone. See if you can spot it: "Abide in me, as I also abide in you. No branch can bear fruit by itself; it must abide in the vine. Neither can you bear fruit unless you abide in me" (v. 4, author paraphrase).

You saw it, didn't you?

Abide.

What does that word mean to you? I want you to start crafting your own working definition today.

Here's what it doesn't mean: trying harder to do more to be a better version of yourself. That's the essence of striving after self-improvement. Abiding in Jesus is the secret to transformation. *Abide.* It's a gentle word. It feels like fellowship. It carries an essence of resting in relationship, living in bonded attachment to Jesus.

Let's circle back to an earlier word from Jesus. I would call this one Jesus's working definition of abiding.

> Are you tired? Worn out? Burned out on religion? Come to me. Get away with me and you'll recover your life. I'll show you how to take a real rest. Walk with me and work with me—watch how I do it. Learn the unforced rhythms of grace. I won't lay anything heavy or ill-fitting on you. Keep company with me and you'll learn to live freely and lightly. (Matt. 11:28–30 MSG)

We will dig in deeper tomorrow.

PRAY

Our Father, thank you for your Son, Jesus. Lord Jesus, yes, you are the true vine, our very source of life. Keep speaking your cleansing word to us. And Father, prune us for greater fruitfulness. Come, Holy Spirit, and bring the abiding presence of Jesus to grow in us. Praying in Jesus's name, amen.

JOURNAL

Are you an activist type, a change agent? Or are you a more passivist type? What would it take to become a "receptive-ist" type of person? And how's that working definition coming?

Maundy Thursday, Day 38

On Receiving Jesus—the New-Creation Life and Releasing the Old-Creation Self

CONSECRATE

Wake up, sleeper, rise from the dead,
and Christ will shine on you. (Eph. 5:14)

Jesus, I belong to you.
I lift up my heart to you.
I set my mind on you.
I fix my eyes on you.
I offer my body to you as a living sacrifice.
Jesus, we belong to you.

Praying in the name of the Father and of the Son and of the Holy Spirit, amen.

READ

Matthew 26:26–28

While they were eating, Jesus took bread, and when he had given thanks, he broke it and gave it to his disciples, saying, "Take and eat; this is my body."

Then he took a cup, and when he had given thanks, he gave it to them, saying, "Drink from it, all of you. This is my blood of the covenant, which is poured out for many for the forgiveness of sins."

CONSIDER

And so we come to the day history and eternity know as Maundy Thursday. *Maundy* comes from the Latin word *mandatum*, meaning "mandate." It comes straight from the celebrated ceremony of Jesus washing his disciples' feet just before the Last Supper. It would also be the night on which Jesus was betrayed by his disciple Judas Iscariot. On this night Jesus gave us a new mandate: "A new command I give you: Love one another. As I have loved you, so you must love one another" (John 13:34).

The secret of transfigured transformation is held by those five words: *As I have loved you.*

We must first receive the love of Jesus, which is to receive Jesus and all he is.

To receive Jesus is to receive light, life, and love.

To receive Jesus is to release darkness, death, and destruction.

Modern Christianity has made the mistake of thinking we must release our brokenness before we can receive Jesus's wholeness. But Jesus doesn't work by replacement. He works by displacement. When he is received, he comes in and pushes out all that is not of him. We receive, and then we can release all that is broken until all that remains is love.

Jesus, you are the secret.

I receive your righteousness and release my sinfulness.

I receive your wholeness and release my brokenness.

I receive your fullness and release my emptiness.

I receive your peace and release my anxiety.

I receive your joy and release my despair.

I receive your courage and release my timidity.

I receive your new-creation life and release my old-creation self.

And on we will go until we are praying our lives and living our prayers . . .

Jesus, I receive your love and release your love, for that will be all that is left of us—for we will have become that which we have beheld—the very love of God in Jesus Christ through the power of the Holy Spirit.

And isn't that what the Lord's Supper is really all about? "This is my body. . . . This is my blood . . . given for you. . . . Do this in remembrance of me." Do what? Receive and release the love of God in Jesus Christ—his body becoming our bodies and our bodies becoming the living sacrifice.

Completely changed into fire!

"And we all, with unveiled face, beholding the glory of the Lord, are being transformed into the same image from one degree of glory to another. For this comes from the Lord who is the Spirit" (2 Cor. 3:18 ESV).

PRAY

Our Father, thank you for your Son, Jesus. Lord Jesus, you are the great giver. Would you make us great receivers? And would you grace us to release everything in us that is not of you? Then you will be all in all and we will be free. We receive your love—your hands washing our feet—and we release your love into the lives of others. We receive your body and blood given for us. By the Holy Spirit, we will release your love in us for others. Praying in your name, amen.

JOURNAL

What do you make of the difference between replacement and displacement? How about the idea of receiving before releasing? Are you ready to receive Jesus and more of Jesus?

Good Friday, Day 39

The Good Friday Question: Is This for Looking At?

CONSECRATE

Wake up, sleeper, rise from the dead,
and Christ will shine on you. (Eph. 5:14)

Jesus, I belong to you.
I lift up my heart to you.
I set my mind on you.
I fix my eyes on you.
I offer my body to you as a living sacrifice.
Jesus, we belong to you.
Praying in the name of the Father and of the Son and of the Holy Spirit, amen.

READ

John 1:29 ESV

The next day he saw Jesus coming toward him, and said, "Behold, the Lamb of God, who takes away the sin of the world!"

CONSIDER

Today we come to the day known to history and eternity as Good Friday.

One of my best and favorite teachers for all his life so far has been my oldest child, David. One day when he was about four, he walked into my study and over to my desk. On the desk was a small figurine of Jesus on the cross, a crucifix. David picked the little statue up and began to study it, turning it over and around in his small hands. Then he asked me this question:

"Dad, what is this? What do we use this for?"

As I prepared to respond to his question, he said these words I will never forget:

"Or, Dad, is this for looking at?"

As he lifted the little statue of Jesus on the cross up in front of his eyes and my eyes, too, I responded, "Yes, David. You are exactly right. This is for looking at."

The secret to the answer to Transformational Question 2, "Do I really want to change?," is all wrapped up in David's answer. The change that is transformation does not come from trying harder to do more to be better. It comes from beholding. "Yes, David, this is for looking at." I cannot change myself. Jesus is the change agent.

John knew it. That day John the Baptist said it best:

"Behold, the Lamb of God, who takes away the sin of the world!"

Sin has us stuck in the brokenness of our fallen selves. We can't get free. Jesus is our freedom. He sets the captives free. Freedom comes through the daily walk of lifting our hearts to him, setting our minds on him, fixing our eyes on him, and offering our bodies to him as a living sacrifice. Beholding Jesus, belonging to Jesus, becoming like Jesus.

We bring the beholding. He brings the change. And what does the change look like? It looks like the movement from darkness to light, from death to life, and from chaos to new creation. It looks like the movement from the slavery of self-interested survival to the freedom of life-giving love. In that light, I think I really want to change.

You may be thinking, *But this feels too easy. This is not how change works.* But what if it is? What if real change is completely different than we thought? What if it is not up to us to do the changing? What if it is up to Jesus? What if transformation is about getting off the treadmill of functional religious activity and finding ourselves perfectly fitted with the yoke of Jesus? And what was it he said about his yoke? I believe his word was "easy."

"The next day again John was standing with two of his disciples, and he looked at Jesus as he walked by and said, 'Behold, the Lamb of God!' The two disciples heard him say this, and they followed Jesus" (John 1:35–37 ESV).

PRAY

Our Father, thank you for your Son, Jesus. Lord Jesus, what joyful freedom it is to know you and to know that the change actually comes from knowing you—belonging to you, beholding you, believing you, and, by your abiding grace, becoming like you. Fill us, Holy Spirit, with the presence of the person of Jesus. Praying in his name, amen.

JOURNAL

What does *beholding* mean to you? How do you behold? What might it mean to shift the focus from your activity to Jesus's person and presence?

Holy Saturday, Day 40

Transformational Question 3

CONSECRATE

Wake up, sleeper, rise from the dead,
and Christ will shine on you. (Eph. 5:14)

Jesus, I belong to you.
I lift up my heart to you.
I set my mind on you.
I fix my eyes on you.
I offer my body to you as a living sacrifice.
Jesus, we belong to you.
Praying in the name of the Father and of the Son and of the Holy Spirit, amen.

READ

Philippians 3:10–11
I want to know Christ—yes, to know the power of his resurrection and participation in his sufferings, becoming like him in his death, and so, somehow, attaining to the resurrection from the dead.

CONSIDER

Now we come to the day known to history and eternity as Holy Saturday. It is the perfect day to come to the final question.

So, back to that day with Maxie. The time had finally come. I was going to learn Transformational Question 3. How did I know? Because Maxie was holding up three fingers across the table from me.

Because Maxie likes to rehearse, he asked me to recount the first two transformational questions:

1. Am I growing?
2. Do I really want to change?

Then he asked, "Are you ready for the third question?"

And without further ado, with no fanfare or drumrolls or further diversions, he dropped the third transformational question like a microphone:

"How deep is my desire for Jesus?"

Although I had given eager and misguided responses to the first two questions, when Maxie asked the third, I just sat there in stunned silence.

How deep is my desire for Jesus?

That word hit soft and then hard—*desire.*

Not duty or discipline, no sense of ought or should. *Desire*. The word *desire* is like a first cousin to the watchword of question 2—*want*. Desire is want touched with holy fire.

Then Maxie gave me the core text of Transformational Question 3: Philippians 3:10–11.

I want to know Christ—yes, to know the power of his resurrection and participation in his sufferings, becoming like him in his death, and so, somehow, attaining to the resurrection from the dead.

If want swims in the current of need, desire dwells in the ocean of love and yes. It inspires the question "How deep?" The old hymn comes to mind:

O the deep, deep love of Jesus,
Vast, unmeasured, boundless, free!
Rolling as a mighty ocean
In its fullness over me.[1]

But the question was "How deep is my desire for Jesus?"

---

1. S. Trevor Francis, "O the Deep, Deep Love of Jesus," in *Our Great Redeemer's Praise*, ed. Jonathan A. Powers (Seedbed, 2022).

Underneath me, all around me
Is the current of Thy love,
Leading onward, leading homeward to
My glorious rest above.[2]

This is a song about Jesus's deep desire for me.

O the deep, deep love of Jesus,
'Tis a heav'n of heav'ns to me,
And it lifts me up to glory,
For it lifts me up to Thee.[3]

And then it hit me: this is the whole point. It's like I am asking Jesus, "How deep is your desire for me?" And he stretches out his arms and motions as he asks, "How high? How deep? How wide? How long?"

O the deep, deep love of Jesus,
Spread His praise from shore to shore!
How He loveth, ever loveth
Changeth never, nevermore.[4]

How deep is my desire for Jesus?

And still wordless, I remembered this ancient word from Mother Julian of Norwich in *Revelations of Divine Love*:

---

2. S. Trevor Francis, "O the Deep, Deep Love of Jesus."
3. S. Trevor Francis, "O the Deep, Deep Love of Jesus."
4. S. Trevor Francis, "O the Deep, Deep Love of Jesus."

> And after this our Lord showed himself more glorified, to my eyes, than I saw Him before. By this I was taught that our soul shall never have rest till it comes to Him, knowing that He is fullness of joy, friendly and courteous, blissful and very life. Our Lord Jesus said again and again, "It is I; it is I; it is I who am highest; it is I whom you love; it is I whom you delight in; it is I whom you serve; it is I whom you long for, whom you desire; it is I whom you mean; it is I who am all."

And then an ocean of tears began to fall.

PRAY

Our Father, thank you for your Son, Jesus. Lord Jesus, on this Holy Saturday, dead and buried in the tomb, you rested from all your work. Thank you for awakening us from our complacency and to the depths of your desire for us. By the power of the Holy Spirit, we declare our deep and ever-deepening desire for you. It is well with our souls. Praying in your name, amen.

JOURNAL

So how deep is your desire for Jesus? Take your time.

Easter Sunday

After the Sabbath, at dawn on the first day of the week, Mary Magdalene and the other Mary went to look at the tomb.

There was a violent earthquake, for an angel of the Lord came down from heaven and, going to the tomb, rolled back the stone and sat on it. His appearance was like lightning, and his clothes were white as snow. The guards were so afraid of him that they shook and became like dead men.

The angel said to the women, “Do not be afraid, for I know that you are looking for Jesus, who was crucified. He is not here; he has risen, just as he said. Come and see the place where he lay. Then go quickly and tell his disciples: ‘He has risen from the dead and is going ahead of you into Galilee. There you will see him.’ Now I have told you.”

So the women hurried away from the tomb, afraid yet filled with joy, and ran to tell his disciples. Suddenly Jesus met them. "Greetings," he said. They came to him, clasped his feet and worshiped him. Then Jesus said to them, "Do not be afraid. Go and tell my brothers to go to Galilee; there they will see me."

—Matthew 28:1–10

An Easter Postscript—
One Last Question

CONSECRATE

Wake up, sleeper, rise from the dead,
and Christ will shine on you. (Eph. 5:14)

Jesus, I belong to you.
I lift up my heart to you.
I set my mind on you.
I fix my eyes on you.
I offer my body to you as a living sacrifice.
Jesus, we belong to you.
Praying in the name of the Father and of the Son and of the Holy Spirit, amen.

READ

Matthew 16:15

"But what about you?" he asked. "Who do you say I am?"

CONSIDER

So how are you responding to the question of all questions?

But what about you? . . . Who do you say that I am?

Let's not make the mistake of just copying down Peter's answer and turning it into the right answer—as though Jesus were just looking for the correct answer.

"You are the Messiah, the Son of the living God" (Matt. 16:16).

The truth is Peter gave Jesus something way beyond a right answer to an important question. Peter offered Jesus a response to divine revelation. Peter did not react to a teacher with a Sunday school answer. He responded to God by leaning in with his life.

Remember my confirmation class from the early days of this Lenten journey? I told them the story of a wire walker who stretched a wire across a treacherous canyon. In front of a stunned audience, he walked across the wire and back. He asked the audience if they thought he could do it again. They cheered loudly with affirmation.

Then he reached for a wheelbarrow and put it on the wire. He asked the cheering audience, "Who will get in the wheelbarrow?"

Faith is not believing the right things about Jesus. Faith is believing Jesus.

If Jesus is the Messiah, the Son of the living God, the Bread of Life and the Light of the World, the Good Shepherd, the way and the truth and the life, very God of very God—and if what is on offer here is to be transformed, to be remade in the image of God, into his likeness—we must respond with our whole lives.

Faith is not the right answer. It is the right response.

When Peter said, "You are the Messiah, the Son of the living God," he was, in essence, responding with the response Jesus had been waiting for: all in.

We asked that question of all questions every single week in our yearlong confirmation class.

It's why I'm asking you, for Jesus, again today.

But what about you? . . . Who do you say that I am?

Don't give the right answer. Respond to the revelation.

I'll never forget how one day, months into our confirmation class, I asked the question of questions, and one of our students, Ava Grace, offered this mind-blowing response to the revelation:

"Where's the wheelbarrow?"

Okay, now it's your turn!

PRAY

Our Father, thank you for your Son, Jesus. Lord Jesus, you are our Lord and our God. Where is the wheelbarrow? We're going all in with you. We are growing. We really want to change. And our desire for you is at an all-time high. Come, Holy Spirit. "Lead on, O King Eternal. The day of march is come.[5] Praying in your name, amen.

JOURNAL

Are you ready to get in the wheelbarrow? Reflect on the Jesus story unfolding in your life these days.

---

5. Ernest W. Shurtleff, "Lead On, O King Eternal," in *Our Great Redeemer's Praise*, ed. Jonathan A. Powers (Seedbed, 2022).

Printed by Libri Plureos GmbH in Hamburg,
Germany

9 798888 002032

JESUS ASKED A LOT OF QUESTIONS. HE STILL DOES.

The world we live in places a premium on answers. Jesus takes a different approach. He's all about the questions. Did you know Jesus asked others upward of three hundred questions in the Gospels? He was asked somewhere in the neighborhood of one hundred eighty questions by others. Interestingly, he only directly answered three of those questions.

What if we pressed pause for a minute on our need for more answers? And what if we upped our game on our quest to find better questions? And isn't this interesting—the connection between *quest* and *question*?

That is the quest of this book. Over the forty days of the season of Lent—in his signature style—J. D. Walt weaves together Scripture and stories to enrich our journey to the cross with Jesus. Starting with what he calls the Question of All Questions—Who do you say that I am?, J. D. unfolds the compelling story of how his mentor taught him three transformational questions. Simple and profound, these questions will awaken your faith and deepen your walk with Jesus.

Whether you are looking for a contemplative personal journey or a shared way with others—even your whole church—*Jesus Asking* will train you in the art of the question and lead you to the answers only God can reveal.

Renowned Bible teacher and prolific author, **JOHN DAVID (J. D.) WALT** is the former dean of chapel of Asbury Theological Seminary and the founder and sower in chief of Seedbed. Seedbed exists to gather, connect, and resource the people of God to sow for a great awakening. He serves as pastor of the Gillett Methodist Church in Gillett, Arkansas.

SOW MUCH MORE AT SEEDBED.COM

ISBN 979-8-88800-203-2
90000
9 798888 002032